John N. Sutl
Lecturer in
Dundee Coll
Bell Street,
Scotland t

Prototyping

The effective use of CASE technology

Prototyping

The effective use of CASE technology

Roland Vonk

Prentice Hall

New York   London   Toronto   Sydney   Tokyo

First published 1990 by
Prentice Hall International (UK) Ltd,
66 Wood Lane End, Hemel Hempstead,
Hertfordshire, HP2 4RG
A division of
Simon & Schuster International Group

© 1990 Roland Vonk; 1987 Academic Service

Printed and bound in Great Britain at
the University Press, Cambridge

Library of Congress Cataloging-in-Publication
Data and British Library Cataloguing in
Publication Data are available from
the publisher.

1   2   3   4   5   93   92   91   90   89

ISBN 0-13-731589-9

To Marjet

Mein Herr looked so thoroughly bewildered that I thought it best to change the subject. 'What a useful thing a pocket-map is!', I remarked.

'That's another thing we've learned from *your* Nation,' said Mein Herr, 'map-making. But we've carried it much further than *you*. What do you consider the *largest* map that would be really useful?'

'About six inches to the mile.'

'Only *six inches*!' exclaimed Mein Herr. 'We very soon got to six *yards* to the mile. Then we tried a *hundred* yards to the mile. And then came the grandest idea of all! We actually made a map of the country, on the scale of a *mile to the mile*!'

'Have you used it much?' I enquired.

'It has never been spread out, yet,' said Mein Herr: 'the farmers objected: they said it would cover the whole country, and shut out the sunlight! So we now use the country itself, as its own map, and I assure you it does nearly as well.'

Lewis Carroll

Contents

Preface

Prototyping is gaining popularity among practitioners and academics working in the field of information systems development. It is now widely accepted that the success of an information system strongly depends on the quality of the system requirements definition, which is drawn up in an early phase of a project. The traditional methods for requirements definition sometimes appear to meet with patchy success. Among the various reasons for this are the shortcomings of diagrams (which are central to many of the popular structured techniques) as a *language for communication* between system developers and users, and the lack of attention of structured methods to the fact that requirements *change* as users gain experience with a system. Prototyping, if applied well, is an effective answer to these problems.

Purpose

In the field of information systems development, prototyping is fairly new. The use of working models of a system, and the explicit iterative nature of the prototyping process, clearly distinguishes it from traditional approaches to requirements definition. Practical experience with this approach is still limited, and a solid theoretical basis still seems to be missing. For these reasons, prototyping projects are generally seen as difficult to plan, budget, execute and control.

This book aims to clarify the prototyping concept by discussing all major facets of this approach to requirements definition. One of its main objectives is to define the concepts and terminology related to prototyping, in order to arrive at a common conceptual framework. This provides the theoretical foundation which is a necessary prerequisite for another objective of the book: to give guidelines for the practical application of prototyping.

As with most other books, many of the thoughts on which this book is based are already in the public domain. The contribution of this book primarily lies in the sharper demarcation of the prototyping concept. Furthermore, unlike many other publications on prototyping, this book provides the reader with a detailed and practical description of this approach to requirements definition.

Structure

The book is in three parts. Part One discusses the 'why, what and when' of prototyping. Among other things, it defines exactly what is meant by the term 'prototyping', characterizes situations suited to a prototyping approach, explains what may and may not be reasonably expected from this approach, and examines the tools that are necessary or desirable for effective prototyping.

Part Two gives guidelines for the practical application of prototyping. It explains how the prototyping principles can be combined with conventional methods for requirements definition to produce a balanced whole. This part of the book should not, however, be read and used as a dogma, but merely as an illustration of the way in which the fundamental principles of prototyping (use of working models, iteration and user participation) can be applied in practice.

Part Three of the book discusses CASE technology. Prototyping is essentially a 'technology-driven' approach. The main reason for the advent and growing popularity of prototyping is the emergence of fourth-generation languages. In order to understand the current limitations and the future of prototyping, it is necessary to have a thorough understanding of the technology which has enabled it to mature.

The three parts are largely independent from one another. In principle, the reader could begin with any part. When necessary, reference is made to subjects discussed in previous parts. However, Part Two (practical application of the prototyping concept) builds on the foundation laid down in Part One. Therefore, the reader is advised to read at least Chapters 3 and 4 of Part One before starting with Part Two.

Terminology

In this book, most of the terms are defined or explained the first time they are used. However, one term, which occurs in the title of the book, should be explained here: 'CASE'.

In the first instance, the term CASE (Computer-Aided System Engineering) was used to refer to automated tools for the information analyst and system designer only. However, since then the term has also been used to refer to program generators and even fourth-generation languages. In this book, I have taken the same broad view of CASE, and use the term in its literal sense to cover all specialized automated tools that support or automate the systems engineering process.

Note also that in this book the masculine form of the personal pronoun has been used. This is for stylistic convenience only, as 'he/she' and similar forms are awkward and irritating.

Title of the book

I have chosen as a title 'Prototyping – the effective use of CASE technology' for two reasons.

First, prototyping and CASE are almost inseparable. Without CASE there would be no prototyping; conversely, prototyping is the most effective way of using CASE technology (and particularly fourth-generation languages). Using fourth-generation tools just as an efficiency-enhancing replacement for third-generation languages simply does not get the full benefits out of this technology.

Secondly, the title is meant to set the reader thinking about the relationship between prototyping and structured methods. Many people associate CASE with structured methods, and regard structured methods and prototyping as incompatible. These readers will probably ask themselves what CASE has to do with prototyping. The relationship between structured methods (and the associated workbenches) and prototyping is one of the main themes of this book.

Audience

This book is addressed to people involved in the development of automated information systems (notably information analysts and designers) and to those with responsibility for the development process. It is meant for both professionals and academics working in the field. It is also expected to be useful in courses on information systems analysis and design in business schools and universities, and in specific training courses in industry. However, it is not in principle intended for end-users, unless they have considerable experience with and interest in analysis and design.

The book is written in a reasonably method-independent style, so knowledge of a particular set of structured methods and techniques is not required. However, some general familiarity with methods and techniques is necessary.

The book is primarily aimed at the field of business information systems. It does not (or only superficially) discuss such things as formal and executable specification languages, the use of Prolog or LISP as prototyping languages, or the use of prototyping in the development of embedded software. Systems suitable for the approach described here are characterized as on-line database-oriented applications, in which the user interface is quite important. However, the concepts discussed may be applied in the field of technical information systems as well.

Acknowledgements

Many people have contributed in many ways to the work presented here. Rien Steenbak and Isaac Eliahou (formerly Philips International b.v.) were the originators of the idea that I should write on the subject of prototyping. Joan Stomps of Academic Service convinced me that it should be a book. The many people that participated in my prototyping classes were a valuable stimulus and aid to the refining of my ideas on the subject.

For their critical remarks on draft versions of the Dutch edition of this book I thank my former colleagues Ad van Riel, Reinier Krooshof, Leo Maarssen and Hans Vermeulen (at the time of writing all colleagues at Philips), and professors Th. M. A. Bemelmans and J. C. Wortmann (Eindhoven University of Technology). For their participation in the review board for the English edition, appreciation is due to Wil van Melis, Wim Swanenburg, Dave Thackwray, Frans Wilbrink and again Ad van xiv *Preface*

Riel. Appreciation is also due to Arno van Abeelen for providing the necessary support and technical means.

Many thanks to Vic Joseph, who made the initial translation. I am greatly indebted to Dave Thackwray, who devoted many tedious hours of his time to the translated version, and did a superb job of improving the text.

I have found that writing a book is a large task. Thanks are due to my relatives and friends for accepting my absence and absent-mindedness during the period. Last, but certainly not least, I would like to thank my wife, Marjet, who had to bear with my frustrations during the process of producing this book.

Roland Vonk

List of Trademarks

ADABAS, NATURAL and PREDICT are trademarks of Software AG.
Apollo is a trademark of Apollo Computer Company.
Apple is a registered trademark of Apple Computer, Inc.
Datamanager is a registered trademark of Manager Software Products, Inc.
Excelerator is a registered trademark of Index Technology Corp.
IBM is a registered trademark of International Business Machines Corp.
IDEAL is a registered trademark of Applied Data Research, Inc.
IDMS is a registered trademark of Cullinet Software, Inc.
IEW is a registered trademark of KnowledgeWare, Inc.
IFPS is a registered trademark of Execucom Systems Corp.
IMS is a trademark of International Business Machines Corp.
Ingres is a trademark of Relational Technology, Inc.
LINC is a registered trademark of UNISYS Corp.
Lotus 1–2–3 is a trademark of Lotus Development Corp.
MAESTRO is a registered trademark of Softlab GmbH.
ManagerView is a trademark of Manager Software Products, Inc.
Mantis is a trademark of Cincom Systems, Inc.
Method/1 is a trademark of Arthur Andersen & Co.
NASTEC CASE2000 is a registered trademark of Nastec Corp.
NOMAD is a product of MUST Software International, Inc.
ProMod is a product of GEI – Gesellschaft für Elektronische
   Informationsverarbeitung MBH.
PSL/PSA is a trademark of Meta Systems, Inc.
RAMIS is a registered trademark of OnLine Software International, Inc.
SADT is a trademark of SofTech, Inc.
SAS is a registered trademark of SAS Institute, Inc.
System W is a trademark of Comshare, Inc.
UNIX is a registered trademark of AT & T.
The Virtual Software Factory is a trademark of The Virtual Software Factory Ltd.
XL/Customizer is a trademark of Index Technology Corp.

Many of the designations used by manufacturers and sellers to distinguish their products are claimed as trademarks. The author has made every attempt to supply trademark information about manufacturers and their products mentioned in this book.

Part One
The Prototyping Concept

Chapter 1

Introduction to Part One

The success of an information system depends strongly on the quality of the system requirements definition, which is drawn up in an early phase of the development project. In spite of all the available structured methods and techniques for requirements definition, it is clearly difficult to discover exactly what the user needs and desires in a system. Traditional modeling techniques often do not appeal very strongly to the average user, and structured methods do not make enough allowance for the learning process which a user goes through when using an information system in practice and for the resulting changed information needs. A consequence of these shortcomings is that an information systems department is often overwhelmed by change requests almost as soon as the new system is installed. There is a clear need for new and more effective approaches for requirements definition.

Prototyping is one such new approach. It is so called because its most prominent characteristic is an extensive use of working models of the system under development, that is, prototypes. In many other disciplines, the construction of prototypes has long been an accepted part of the process of developing new products. Until recently, the construction of prototype information systems was not feasible, because of the lack of powerful development tools. However, the advancing automation of the systems development process is bringing changes to this area. CASE tools are having radical consequences for the way in which information systems can and should be developed.

Part One of this book discusses the prototyping concept and a number of related issues. Among other things, it defines the term 'prototyping', characterizes situations suited to a prototyping approach, explains what may and may not reasonably be expected from this approach, and examines the tools that are necessary or desirable to make effective prototyping possible. Viewing Part One chapter by chapter, we can summarize its contents as follows.

Chapter 2 describes a number of the problems confronting application systems developers, and explores ways in which these problems can be tackled. It aims to position prototyping in relation to other new approaches to systems development and to make clear why the prototyping approach is an indispensable part of any program of measures for increasing the productivity of the systems development staff.

Chapter 3 defines the concepts 'prototype' and 'prototyping'. There is much terminological confusion in this area. In this book, prototyping is regarded as an approach for requirements definition. The purpose of a prototype is to bring into focus specific aspects of the system; it is not intended to function faultlessly in practice, and should therefore never be deployed as it stands as a production system. This chapter also explores a number of other terms related to prototyping.

Chapter 4 characterizes the problem situations in which prototyping may be particularly useful. When the prototype is retained as the basis of the production system prototyping will almost always be cost-effective. On the other hand, where the prototype is discarded at the end of the prototyping process the main tangible value of prototyping is that it reduces uncertainty about the information problem. A thorough analysis of this problem must then reveal whether it entails significant uncertainty, and thus whether prototyping is cost-effective. Chapter 4 also summarizes the conditions which must be satisfied before a prototyping approach can be applied.

Chapter 5 deals with the problems which may be encountered during prototyping, and the ways in which such problems may be avoided. It also describes the pitfalls to avoid when introducing prototyping into an organization.

Finally, Chapter 6 contains some brief concluding remarks. In particular, the chapter draws attention to the lack of empirical material on the effects of prototyping, and mentions a number of topics which are candidates for further research.

Chapter 2

Meeting the Organization's Information Needs

An efficient and reliable information infrastructure, which ensures that the right information is available in the right place at the right time, has a powerful influence on the decisiveness and effectiveness of an organization. More and more organizations are realizing the value of information. The idea that it is an asset equal in importance to capital, materials and labor has taken root. In present practice, however, the organizational unit responsible for the development of new (automated) information systems is frequently incapable of meeting the end-user's information needs adequately and with sufficient speed.

In this chapter, the problems confronting the typical information systems department are briefly examined in Section 2.1. In Sections 2.2 and 2.3, we describe some measures to deal with these problems. Section 2.2 looks at two alternatives to the traditional approach to system development. In Section 2.3 we describe some ways of raising the productivity of system development personnel. Section 2.4 summarizes the chapter.

2.1 THE 'SOFTWARE CRISIS'

Everyone currently involved in the development of information systems is vexed by the seemingly intractable problems of the 'software crisis'. Development activities (analysis, design and programming) usually take far too long, certainly when viewed from the standpoint of a user waiting for the system. It seems almost inevitable that projects overrun planned completion dates, and that development costs are a multiple of those estimated. When the information system is finally handed over to its users, it is not unusual for the system to need thorough revision after a short period of operation.

Maintenance of existing applications makes such substantial demands on the information systems department's capacity that the department hardly has time to develop new applications. It is common for as much as 80 per cent of the total capacity to be expended on maintenance. As a result, the length of the *application backlog* (the portfolio of requests for development) demoralizes the users. Delays in the development of new or revised systems in excess of three years are common. In a study by IBM (Xephon, 1983), it was reported that 33 per cent of clients had to contend with such delays; Martin (1982a) describes a large bank with a backlog of seven years.

It is clear that such situations lead to ill-will between end-users and the information systems department. A further serious consequence of this is the *invisible application backlog*: disillusioned users cease to even consider asking for applications, which are sometimes in fact strategically indispensable. In a 1981 study by the Sloan School of Management, in a typical Fortune 500 corporation the invisible backlog was 1.68 times as large as the registered one (Rosenberger, 1981). In respect of management information systems, Alloway and Quillard (1983) established that, typically, the demand for such systems was 2.5 to 3 times as great as the portfolio of systems approved for development.

It seems that this situation has not improved, and people are assiduously searching for avenues of escape from these problems. Fortunately, recent developments in both technology and methodology offer all sorts of possible solutions. Measures for solving the kinds of problem described above can be broadly classified into two groups: firstly, measures which reduce the amount of work the information systems department has to do (Section 2.2), and secondly, measures to raise the productivity of system developers (Section 2.3).

2.2 ALTERNATIVE DEVELOPMENT APPROACHES

Many information problems can be solved either by letting end-users develop the necessary information system or by using application packages. Sometimes these approaches are more effective than those in which the information systems department follows the traditional development route. Both alternative development strategies are briefly discussed in this section.

2.2.1 End-user computing

The current availability of a large number of user-friendly software tools (such as Lotus123, Nomad and SAS) has led to a situation in which end-users may be able to develop a necessary application quickly by themselves (Martin, 1982a). Sometimes – for example when a user needs data from a production database – professional support in this activity is essential. In a growing number of organizations, this support can be found in the Information Centre, whose functions include propagating and stimulating end-user computing, and offering accompanying professional support (see Wetherbe and Leitheiser, 1985, for example).

End-user computing has, indisputably, many advantages. Misunderstandings caused by faulty communication between user and developer disappear; the user and system developer are one and the same. The point in time at which the system is ready for use no longer depends on existing priorities in the information systems department so, in general, applications will be ready sooner. The information systems department's load is lightened, and the department can concentrate on those applications for which a professional approach is a prerequisite.

However, not every information problem lends itself to end-user computing. For example, the approach is not generally suited to large or multi-user systems. Neither is it suited to systems that modify data in an operational database, since these applications potentially put the integrity (consistency, completeness) of the database at risk. In each problem situation it is necessary to decide, on the basis of such criteria, whether development by end-users is permissible or wise.[1]

We may conclude that, although some applications can be developed better and more quickly by end-users than by the information systems department, a large number of applications will still demand a professional approach and will continue to fall within the responsibility of this department.

2.2.2 Application packages

A second strategy for reducing the amount of work to be done by the information systems department is the use of standard application packages. When the activities to be supported by the information system are common to many organizations, there is a strong possibility that the information problem can be solved by packaged software (Gremillion and Pyburn, 1983). This applies, for instance, to a great many administrative applications (general ledger, accounts receivable and payable, salary and personnel administration), and to applications in the logistics field (for example implementations of the materials requirements planning (MRP) concept). The number of packages available in many areas is growing rapidly; the quality of these packages shows an upward trend and prices are falling (Diebold Group, 1983).

Buying a package is usually much less expensive than in-house development of the application. Furthermore, the system will be available more quickly, in particular because of a dramatic reduction in the necessary programming time. The degree to which such benefits accrue, however, directly depends on the extent to which the package satisfies the requirements and wishes of the end-users. The match will be exact in only a tiny proportion of cases – generally, either the package or the procedures in the organization will have to be modified. Prior to the purchase of a standard application package, an estimate of the costs associated with these inevitable modifications must be made. It is clear that this kind of evaluation can be sensibly made only when there is a clear picture of the requirements and wishes of the future users of the package, and when these requirements and wishes are stable (Flint *et al.*, 1983).

Other considerations are the relatively limited flexibility and the dependence on the supplier which are (with a few exceptions) associated with the package approach. Often, after a few years, an initially acceptable package comes to be felt as a straitjacket. As soon as modifications that were not anticipated by the supplier of the package are needed, the organization is faced with extremely high costs. If the source code is available and the organization makes structural changes, the supplier is usually no longer prepared to take responsibility for maintaining the package. One of the main advantages of the standard package approach is thereby nullified. Nevertheless, this situation is changing somewhat with the arrival of packages written (partly) in a fourth-generation language (see also Section 2.3.1.2). These are usually easier to modify or extend than those written in COBOL.

A detailed survey of the considerations which play a role in buying a standard package can be found in Diebold Group (1983). Apart from these considerations, an organization sometimes nevertheless decides (for example for competitive reasons) to take its own, unique approach, even when the problem is a fairly standard one for which application packages are probably obtainable.

To sum up, it can be seen that the utilization of standard application packages can make a real contribution to solving the problems described in Section 2.1. This approach has, however, a number of drawbacks. These include the generally restricted flexibility, making this strategy an unsuitable choice in situations where there is uncertainty about the requirements with regard to the system to be developed.

2.3 IMPROVING SYSTEM DEVELOPMENT PRODUCTIVITY

In this book, the term 'productivity' is understood as the magnitude of the effectively solved problem per unit of time invested. Productivity thus relates both to the efficiency of the development process and to the effectiveness of the developed product. The efficiency aspect refers to the cost (in time and money) of realizing an information system. Pursuing an efficient process means attempting to realize the product at the lowest possible effort. The second aspect – product effectiveness – refers to the extent to which an information system satisfies the real information needs of its users. (Note that the term 'productivity' has often been used in a narrower sense by others referring only to the efficiency of the development process.)

In the remainder of this section, ways of increasing the efficiency of the development process will be discussed, followed by an investigation of measures which can be taken to improve the effectiveness of that process.

2.3.1 Raising the efficiency of the development process

Self-evident measures for raising the efficiency of the development process are the use of automated tools to support the development tasks, and automation of these tasks. In this context, the term CASE will often be encountered in current literature.

At first, this term was used only to refer to automated tools for supporting structured methods and techniques. However, the use of the term in the market-place has multiplied rapidly and COBOL generators and even fourth-generation language products are now also described by their suppliers as 'CASE' products. In this connection, a distinction is sometimes drawn nowadays between 'upper CASE' products (software tools for the requirements definition and design phases) and 'lower CASE' products (software tools for the realization phase). In this book, we use the term CASE to cover all the specialized tools that are intended to support or automate the systems engineering process. Section 2.3.1.1 briefly introduces the subject workbenches and IPSEs (see below), and Section 2.3.1.2 takes a look at fourth-generation languages. Part Three of this book goes into detail about both subjects.

2.3.1.1 Workbenches and IPSEs

The majority of currently available development tools aim to support activities in the realization stage of the development project. The programmer can nowadays select from a veritable arsenal of compilers/interpreters, linkers, debuggers, editors, etc. The number of tools to support activities in the other phases of a project is growing very rapidly as is the interest being taken in this kind of tool.

Among the first tools supporting the requirements definition or design phase were PSL/PSA (from University of Michigan; Teichroew and Hershey, 1977), SREM (from TRW; Bell *et al.*, 1977) and AUTOIDEF (from Boeing; Smith *et al.*, 1980). In the first instance, tools of this kind were implemented on mainframes. Running costs were high and the response times were poor. Because these tools generally made use of DVST screens (direct-view storage tubes, or memory tubes), the user was confronted with a very unfriendly, and sometimes downright unusable, interface. Consequently, over busy communication lines it took a very long time to build up a complete diagram.

Minicomputers and especially microcomputers offer much greater potential for achieving genuinely user-friendly software tools. Examples of early tools available on such hardware are Intech's Excelerator (Umeh, 1985), GEI's PROMOD (Hruschka, 1983), and Nastec's CASE2000 (Kull, 1985). Typically, these tools offer a well-designed user interface, advanced graphics facilities and response times that are quite acceptable.

In many cases, software tools support narrowly defined tasks. Combining tools to cover a greater part of the systems engineering process is difficult: the various tools show overlap, cannot easily communicate with one another and have different user interfaces. However, there is a growing awareness that the extent to which a tool can be integrated with others strongly influences its usefulness. Increasingly, sets of tools closely attuned to one another are becoming available. These sets are often referred to as 'workbenches'. Depending on the kind of activities supported, they may be known as 'analyst workbenches', 'designer's workbenches', 'programmer's workbenches' or 'project management workbenches' (EDP Analyzer, 1985). A good example of an analyst workbench is Excelerator. An example of a programmer's workbench is PWB/UNIX (from Bell Telephone Laboratories), which offers programmers working in the UNIX environment a consistent, coherent and powerful set of facilities (Diebold Group, 1982; Hausen and Mullerburg, 1982).

An acronym that the reader may frequently encounter in the literature is 'IPSE' (Integrated Project Support Environment) (Mair, 1986). An IPSE consists of an integrated set of tools for all the activities which take place within a project. It thus in fact contains an integrated set of workbenches for both developers (analysts, designers and programmers) and the project management.

The term 'IPSE' is, at present, mainly used in the technical automation sector (real-time, embedded systems). By far the largest proportion of current IPSEs has evolved from programming support environments for languages used primarily in the technical sector. The majority of IPSEs have therefore been realized on Digital, Sun or Apollo equipment, which are used primarily in the technical area. The terms 'analyst workbench' and 'CASE' are most popular with people working with business information systems. Analyst workbenches are therefore generally realized on IBM or IBM-compatible equipment. The suppliers of analyst workbenches increasingly strive to provide integrated sets of tools to support all phases and all activities of a project – in other words (but usually not yet named as such) IPSEs.

When IPSEs and analyst workbenches are mentioned in this book, it is not intended to refer specifically to tools for use in either the technical or the business area. Although these terms originated in the respective areas of technical software and business information systems, the concepts they stand for are equally valid in both. Furthermore, the term 'analyst workbench' will be used in this book to refer to both analyst and designer workbenches. Of course, analysts and designers use different methods, but the facilities which a workbench must include to support the two types of method are, for all practical purposes, identical. The dividing line between an analyst workbench and a designer's workbench cannot always be clearly drawn, and the term 'designer's workbench' is rarely used, in either the industry or the literature.

Finally, it must be noted that the IPSE concept, however popular it may be, is in fact too narrow. As the acronym suggests, the explicit aim of an IPSE is project support. What is really needed is an integrated set of tools to support all systems engineering tasks, including those outside the scope of the development project itself. In particular, support is also required for:

1. Activities that precede system development (information planning).
2. Activities that follow system development (maintenance).
3. Related activities such as data administration.

It seems useful to introduce a term which completely covers the required development environment. We have chosen the term 'Integrated Systems Engineering Environment' (ISEE).

2.3.1.2 Fourth-generation languages

Analyst workbenches aim primarily at supporting the system developer during the early phases of a development project. This is still, relatively speaking, virgin territory. As already discussed, so far much more attention has been paid to the automation of the development activities which take place later in the development project. These activities are relatively easy to formalize and have thus been obvious candidates for automation. This has led to the appearance of numerous fourth-generation languages. These languages will be dealt with in detail in Part Three; the description here will be limited to a few main features.

The common characteristic of fourth-generation languages is that they relieve the programmer of a great deal of concern about procedural aspects. Languages of the first three generations (machine code, assembler and high-level languages) require the developer to indicate with extreme accuracy and detail the process by which a specific result must be achieved. In a fourth-generation language, however, the developer describes what the process must achieve, rather than the process itself (the actions which must lead to the result). In comparison with third-generation languages, fourth-

(a) LIST employee.name, employee.salary
    WHERE employee.department = "Sales"

(b) <Open file employees>
    <print a report heading and date>
    <get the first employee record>
    Matching_Employee_Found:=FALSE
    WHILE FOUND
    DO   BEGIN
                    IF department = "Sales"
                    THEN BEGIN
                            WRITELN<name, salary>
                            Matching_Employee_Found:=TRUE
                          END
                    <get the next employee record>
            END
    IF Matching_Employee_Found=FALSE
    THEN WRITELN<"No records found">
    <Close file employees>

Figure 2.1 Program fragments in (*a*) a non-procedural and (*b*) a procedural language.

generation languages are more problem oriented, or non-procedural. In the fourth generation it is the task of the compiler or interpreter to solve the procedural problems.

By way of illustration, Fig. 2.1 compares a program written in a fictitional non-procedural language with one that accomplishes the same task but is written in some conventional procedural programming language. Both programs produce a report listing the names and salaries of all employees in the sales department. If no employees are found then a report heading is printed, together with a message 'no records found'.

The non-procedural nature of fourth-generation languages means that the flexibility and reliability of applications programmed in these languages are considerably increased. This is because a great deal of the manual, and thus error prone, programming work is taken over by the compiler/interpreter. The developer can thus concentrate on describing the desired result, without being distracted by such irrelevant considerations as the program control flow.

The use of fourth-generation languages can lead to a considerable increase in the efficiency of the development process. This effect is further intensified in those cases where the language is part of an integrated development environment (consider ADR/ Ideal, for example). All the tools in this kind of environment communicate with one another via a data dictionary. A modification has to be made only once, after which every tool uses the new definition. All the components of such an environment have a uniform interface with the user, allowing him to switch rapidly from one tool to another without leaving the development environment. Inevitably, this has a highly beneficial effect on the efficiency of the development process. Rudolph (1983)

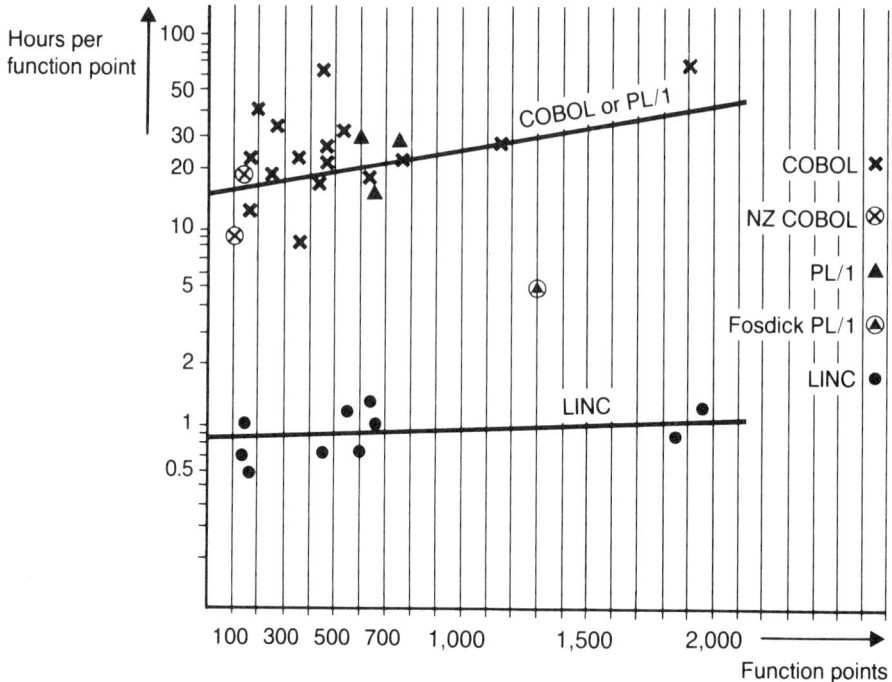

Figure 2.2 Number of function points produced per hour using third-generation and fourth-generation languages. (*Source*: Rudolph (1983). Reprinted with permission.)

established that when using the Unisys fourth-generation language, LINC, 20 to 50 times as many function points[2] per unit of time are produced as when COBOL is used (see Fig. 2.2). This, incidentally, is one of the few studies cited in the literature that provides an objective measurement of increase in productivity. Other authors talk of even more spectacular rises in productivity but generally in these cases a subjective estimate is involved.

The chief conclusion to be drawn from these sections is that there are many aids now available for improving the efficiency with which development activities are carried out – in other words, for raising the productivity of the developer. The application of CASE technology will certainly contribute to reducing the set of problems currently faced by the automation world.

2.3.2 Increasing the effectiveness of the development process

In the pursuit of greater productivity, raising the effectiveness of the development process is even more important than increasing its efficiency. It makes little sense to develop an information system in an exceptionally efficient way when the product is itself of little or no use. The effectiveness of the development process is significantly related to the quality of the system requirements definition. A system requirements

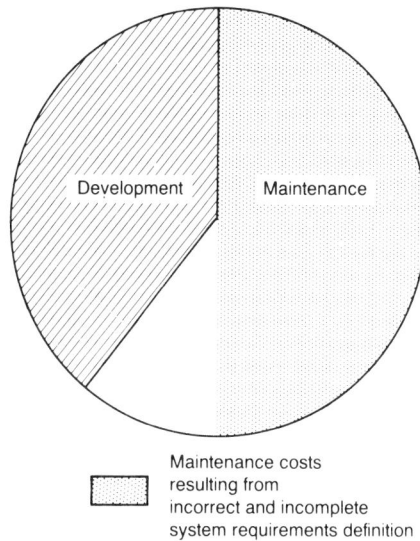

Figure 2.3 Costs resulting from an incorrect or incomplete requirements definition.

definition may be regarded as a contract between the developers and the users, describing exactly what requirements the users lay down for the system that is to be developed. A hazily formulated collection of requirements and wishes, with inconsistencies, ambiguities and omissions, forms a poor basis for the design and construction of an information system, and will undoubtedly result in the completed system being ineffective – that is, failing to meet the end-users' requirements and wishes.

In an early study by Lientz *et al.* (1978) it was found that, typically, only 20 to 40 per cent of the total maintenance effort associated with an information system relates to fixing bugs and to adapting the software to a changing (technical) environment; the greater part of the maintenance costs (60 to 80 per cent) is a direct consequence of errors and ambiguities in the system requirements definition. Since it is widely accepted that the total maintenance costs form approximately 60 per cent of the total life-cycle costs (development and maintenance costs together), it may be concluded that between 35 and 50 per cent of the total life-cycle costs of an information system are caused by the low quality of the system requirements definition (Fig. 2.3). Thus, in many cases, the maintenance costs resulting from incorrectly or incompletely defined requirements exceed the development costs of the information system.

It will thus be clear that increasing the quality of the system requirements definition can lead to considerable savings, which are even greater than those achievable through measures aimed at raising the efficiency of the development process.

2.3.2.1 Structured methods and techniques
The first measure aimed at increasing the quality of the system requirements definition is the use of structured development methods and techniques. This remark may look like forcing an open door, but in more places than might at first be expected such

development methods and techniques are used either not at all or incorrectly. Yourdon (1986) estimated that only 10 per cent of North American companies apply structured methods in a disciplined way.

There are a number of reasons for this limited use. First, too much value is often attached to the time at which programming can be started (Baber, 1982). The longer the requirements definition phase lasts, the more management feels uneasy because there is not much in the way of a tangible product to be seen. This is epitomized in the 'WHISCY' syndrome – Why Isn't Sam Coding Yet? The system developers themselves sometimes regard the system requirements definition as a delaying burden. They see the accurate documentation of all the requirements, wishes, preferences and assumptions as the most tiresome part of the development process, and sometimes even believe they can do without a detailed requirements definition. Management, developers and users are often unaware of the considerable extent to which the quality of the system requirements definition influences the success of the project.

Secondly, it must be realized that the introduction of structured methods and techniques into an organization demands much time, money and effort. Developers will have to learn how to use the methods, and for this it is insufficient simply to attend a single training course. It may take years before an organization is really permeated by the development process philosophy which underlies the method. Organizations often display a large degree of inertia; the introduction of new ways of working and thinking is generally accompanied by the typical problems associated with any process of change.

Thirdly, there are a number of practical obstacles which impede the correct use of structured methods. Specifications, particularly early in the requirements definition phase, have not stabilized (Davis, 1982). The repeated manual composition and revision of diagrams, texts, tables, lists, etc. consumes so much time that information analysts are inclined to put off making the documentation until there are no more changes to be expected. Moreover, a great deal of effort is required to keep the requirements definition consistent. There are often a large number of sometimes obscure connections between the various parts of a requirements document. Diagrams are strongly mutually coupled; modification of one diagram can have many different unanticipated consequences on a large number of other diagrams, both at the same and at different levels of abstraction. Detecting these consequences is extremely time consuming, and it is often not possible to perform this task satisfactorily. As a result of these practical problems, information analysts who try to apply structured methods and techniques properly sometimes do not get round to analyzing the information problem.

The introduction of structured methods and techniques into an organization can only succeed when management, developers and users are fully conscious of the importance of a structured approach. In many cases this demands a substantial change of attitude. The practical problems associated with the use of structured methods and techniques will have to be resolved by the acquisition of automated tools that support the methods in use. Analyst workbenches provide support in preserving consistency and completeness in the analysis and design data, and they help in the maintenance of the documentation produced. Although workbenches primarily aim at increasing the efficiency of the development process, they also have a real influence on its effectiveness. The raised efficiency means that activities which were previously too time consuming now become feasible, enabling structured methods to be properly applied. This generally results in significantly better system requirements definitions and, thus, in more effective systems.

2.3.2.2 *Prototyping*

The application of structured methods and techniques for requirements definition will not however always lead to the much-needed increase in effectiveness. Often, the organization is faced with a considerable maintenance burden, despite using structured methods and associated workbenches. This is because structured methods are based on assumptions which are not always valid. They assume that the diagrams produced by the current development techniques provide an adequate channel of communication between developers and users, and that users' needs remain stable after the traditional requirements definition process. These two assumptions are critically examined in the following paragraphs.

COMMUNICATION PROBLEMS

There is a wide communication gap between the world of automation professionals and that of end-users. The creation of a data processing system is a complex process in which a great deal of attention must be paid to technical aspects. Of necessity, the information systems department is strongly technically oriented in its work, and uses a language adapted to its own activities (a phenomenon which also occurs in any other specialist discipline). To the layman, this jargon is largely incomprehensible. Although the terms that end-users employ are less exotic than those common in the automation world, users also have their own jargon. It is hardly surprising that there are severe communication problems between system developers and users.

The need to improve communication was an important motivation for the development of many strongly graphics-oriented modeling techniques, such as the activity diagrams associated with SofTech's SADT (Marca and McGowan, 1988) and ISAC (Lundeberg *et al.*, 1981). The expectation was that such diagramming techniques would result in a common language. Although in some cases this aim has been achieved, it must be said that the undertaking has not generally been very successful. One cause of this is that learning such a new language demands too much time from the busy user. More important, however, is that the functional description of an information system, even when represented in a diagrammatic form, is still too abstract and difficult for the average user to interpret. It appears that users are unable to understand the information system on the basis of such a description.

To some extent, this difficulty may be due to lack of the necessary skills on the user's part. In contrast to the information analyst, many end-users do not have the experience and knowledge necessary to deal with the abstractions which professional developers are used to handling. Further, they are not acquainted with the numerous design alternatives and their implications. The relationship between user and information analyst is similar to that between a house buyer and an architect; the layman usually has only a sketchy understanding of the architect's drawings, and becomes aware of what he really wants only after he has moved in. Part of the problem may also be ascribed to the medium. It appears it is practically impossible to communicate the dynamic character of a system clearly by means of a static description. Interactive systems demand interactive specifications (Boar, 1984). If a picture is worth a thousand words, then a working model is worth a thousand pictures!

LACK OF ATTENTION FOR THE USER INTERFACE

Many of the currently popular methods, such as Yourdon's Structured Design, and SofTech's SADT, pay no attention to modeling the user interface of a system (screen and report layouts, and dialogue structure). They provide the analyst with the means to model the functions the system has to perform, the structure of the database, and so on, but typically they do not include any techniques for modeling the interaction between the user and the system. So, a system requirements definition made with the help of methods such as these does not give future users of the system any clue about how the system will look and feel. Techniques which model the system's external appearance on paper constitute a step in the right direction, but they still give the user only a static picture of a dynamic system.

The limited attention paid to modeling the user interface by the present generation of requirements definition methods gives some cause for concern. In the last few years, there has been a major shift from batch to interactive applications. The user interface has become increasingly important. Industry surveys indicate that, in a typical database application, around 50 per cent of the coding effort is spent on the realization of input/output routines (Horowitz *et al.*, 1985). For some obscure reason, the 'What-You-See-Is-What-You-Get' principle has not yet penetrated to the area of information systems development. Amazingly, users accept this situation.

INSTABILITY OF INFORMATION NEEDS

In the 'traditional' way of developing information systems, a development project is divided into a number of fairly standard phases. The preliminary investigation is followed by the requirements definition phase, in which a complete and detailed overview of all the requirements and wishes of the system's future users has to be produced. This overview must be rigorous, since the early detection of defects can result in considerable savings. Here, too, prevention is better than cure: in the realization and operational phases, repairing errors caused by ambiguities or mistakes in the requirements definition may consume up to 100 times more effort than immediate correction (Boehm, 1981). Building on the basis of the system requirements definition there follows the design and realization of the information system. The user's first real confrontation with the system is during the acceptance test. Until then it has existed for him only on paper.

This approach implicitly assumes that a user is capable of indicating in detail both what information the system has to produce and in what form during the requirements definition phase. We may reasonably doubt the validity of this assumption. Experience shows that in this phase the users are often very uncertain about both the functions they wish to have present in the system and the form the system must eventually take. Often the user has a clear idea of what is actually wanted only after working with the system for a while. A learning process takes place for which the traditional approach to system development makes no allowance. The new information need resulting from this learning process manifests itself as a large number of change requests.

This is clearly a failing of the traditional development approach, and of the methods used during the requirements definition phase. The conclusion sometimes drawn from this in the literature – that there is 'thus' an obvious need for even more rigorous methods of describing the information requirement (by representing it in a formal language) – is incorrect. A really effective approach to the process of determining the information needs must make allowance for the evolution in those needs that almost inevitably takes place as the user gains experience with the system.

A NEW APPROACH: PROTOTYPING

To summarize the previous section: the traditional modeling techniques for requirements definition fall short as a language of communication between developers and users, and often pay no attention to modeling the user interface of a system. Further, traditional analysis methods do not sufficiently anticipate the evolution of the information needs which takes place as users gain experience with the system.

A consequence of these deficiencies is that the use of structured methods and techniques often fails to provide the anticipated results – complete and accurate specifications of the information system to be developed. Structured methods and techniques are certainly useful as analysis and documentation aids for the developer, but they are less suitable for communication between developers and users. As a result, the user often commits himself, by signing a requirements document, to a requirements definition whose full implications he cannot possibly understand. Often this document is discovered to be full of ambiguities, errors and omissions – hardly a good basis for further development.

Some innovation to complement the existing approaches and methods for requirements definition and to cure the obvious shortcomings is therefore urgently required. *Prototyping* seems to provide an effective answer to the problems that are observed. One characteristic of the prototyping approach is the extensive use of working models as a means of communication between developers and users. A second, novel aspect of prototyping is its strongly iterative character. Prototyping supports and recognizes the learning process undergone by users as they gain experience with a system. On the basis of prototype versions of the information system, the user can empirically establish the real requirements for the system.

Prototyping most certainly does not imply a return to the ways of working which prevailed before the 'structured revolution' (i.e. the introduction of methods and techniques which brought structure into the development process). Structured methods and techniques are also used in prototyping. Part Two provides a detailed description of the way in which traditional methods are applied within the iterative and heuristic prototyping process.

2.4 SUMMARY

In seeking solutions to the problems of the 'software crisis' there are two (by no means mutually exclusive) routes that can be taken: aiming to reduce the number of applications that have to be developed by the information systems department, and aiming to improve the productivity of systems professionals.

Some applications can be developed more quickly and better by the end-users themselves (Section 2.2.1); other information problems can be solved by using standard application packages (Section 2.2.2). Other applications are of such great importance to the organization that a professional approach is essential. The creation of such information systems should remain the responsibility and task of the information systems department.

Increased productivity can be realized in two ways: by raising either the efficiency of the development process or its effectiveness. The efficiency of the development process can be increased by automating it to the greatest possible extent. In this connection, we referred to analyst workbenches and fourth-generation development environments (Section 2.3.1). In Section 2.3.2, however, we noted that measures aimed at increasing the effectiveness of the development process have a greater effect than those aimed at increasing its efficiency. We also noted that the effectiveness of the development process is particularly dependent on the quality of the system requirements definition.

Where methods and techniques for the structured development of information systems are not yet used (or well used), their deployment will, in itself, lead to a considerable improvement in the quality of the system requirements definition. If the methods and techniques are properly supported by automated tools, the modeling techniques associated with them are a powerful aid to analysis, and the diagrams produced make good documentation. These diagrams are, moreover, an excellent means of mutual communication among developers. However, traditional methods fall short as a means of communication between developers and end-users, and typically pay scant attention to the user interface. They also make insufficient allowance for the changes that take place in information needs when the end-users are confronted with the system and obtain experience in using it. The information systems department will frequently be faced with a considerable maintenance burden in spite of having made use of structured methods and techniques.

Prototyping is an approach which counters the deficiencies of traditional methods. If the aim is to raise the productivity of the systems development function, prototyping offers excellent prospects. Although prototyping probably does not help to speed the development of systems (see Chapter 4), the final result will certainly be more effective than with systems realized in the traditional manner.

Those organizations that profit fully from the new developments taking place in methodology and technology are unquestionably in a position to create a properly functioning and flexible information infrastructure. The organization's decisiveness and effectiveness, and hence its competitive position, depend directly on the quality of this infrastructure.

NOTES

1. For an extensive survey of the criteria to be used, see for instance Shomenta *et al.* (1983).
2. Function points measure the functionality supplied to the user. They are calculated by 'Function Point Analysis' (FPA), a technique developed at IBM by A. Albrecht (1979).

Chapter 3

Prototyping – Concepts and Terminology

There is hardly a professional journal in the automation field which has not published a paper on prototyping. In spite of all this attention, progress in this area is still rather slow. One of the main reasons for this is the lack of consensus on what prototyping is or should be. Different authors use different definitions; frequently researchers and writers on the subject do not define the concept explicitly at all. As synonyms are also in use, the literature on prototyping is not exactly transparent.

This chapter describes in detail what we mean by 'prototype' and 'prototyping'. Sections 3.1 and 3.2 give the definitions, and are followed by a more detailed explanation of the prototyping concept.

3.1 THE TERM 'PROTOTYPE'

In this book, a prototype is defined as:

a working model of (parts of) an information system, which emphasizes specific aspects of that system.

Central to this definition is the 'model' concept. In a prototype there is no question of an attempt at completeness; its function is to throw light on specific aspects of the information system. There will be particular emphasis on those aspects about which there is most uncertainty.

As explained in Chapter 2, various modeling methods and techniques are already in use during the development of information systems. The essential difference between prototypes and models produced using such methods and techniques is expressed in the definition by the word 'working'. In general, a prototype will act or look like the system it is intended to model. Visible differences between the prototype and the aspects or parts of the information system it models will be quite limited. A prototype is not merely a representation of the system on paper, but a genuinely usable model of it, implemented on a computer. Prototypes are evaluated by allowing end-users to obtain practical experience of the system. This is, of course, impossible with the traditional kinds of model, which represent the functional properties of an information system in a fairly abstract graphical or formal language.

Prototypes come in all shapes and sizes. Sometimes a prototype models only the external appearance of a system (screens, reports, dialogues), and no action is taken with any data input by the user. This kind of prototype is often termed a *mock-up* of the information system. In other cases, the prototype also allows the user to store data and to perform operations on these data. Such prototypes are generally (and also in this book) called *functional prototypes*. Some prototypes are very comprehensive, and model highly complex systems; others model relatively simple and small systems. A prototype may model either only a part of the system to be developed, or the entire system.

A clear distinction must be made between a prototype and a *production system*. Production systems are intended for operational use, so it follows that stringent demands are generally made on quality (reliability, robustness, maintainability, performance, etc.). Prototypes, in contrast, aim to provide clarification by visualizing those aspects of a system about which there is uncertainty. Prototypes are used to verify the accuracy of the assumptions made about those aspects. In contrast to production systems, prototypes are typically incomplete, and are not intended to function faultlessly.

In many branches of engineering, the use of prototypes is common practice. The construction of prototypes in the car or aircraft industry is a routine part of the development process for new products. In these environments, different kinds of prototype are used to visualize diverse aspects of the product under development. However, there is one kind of prototype often made in a manufacturing environment but not in the development of information systems: during the later stages of the product development cycle a complete version of the product or one of its components – a 'real-life' prototype – is often constructed. The only difference between this kind of prototype and the final product is the way in which it is manufactured.

In the case of a product such as a car, the manufacturing process itself is a costly affair, and the product will be sold in large quantities, thus aggravating the financial consequences of any design errors. The high cost of developing a real-life prototype is therefore justified. In information systems, what might be called a 'real-life' prototype is, in fact, a finished system. Modifying such a prototype would be as costly as modifying a production system and little would be gained. In the field of information systems engineering, labelling of a finished system as a prototype is sometimes a veiled way of indicating that the project has, perhaps, not really achieved all its objectives. By this misuse of the term, developers excuse themselves in advance for future problems.

In the case of application packages, which are intended for reproduction in large quantities, it may well make economic sense to make a fully working system with the intention of pilot testing it. However, for the sake of clarity, we propose to use the term 'pilot system' in this case, and to reserve the term 'prototype' exclusively for use in the context of prototyping as defined in the next section. It will there become clear that prototyping is an activity of a very different nature from pilot testing a practically finished information system.

3.2 THE TERM 'PROTOTYPING'

Unlike the widely used and well-understood term 'prototype', the term 'prototyping' is one that will be familiar only to those working in the field of information system development. This term has acquired a specific, distinctive meaning in the automation field. We define prototyping as:

> *an approach for establishing a systems requirements definition which is characterized by a high degree of iteration, by a very high degree of user participation in the development process and by an extensive use of prototypes.*

The prototyping approach represents a new outlook on how best to arrive at a definition of the system requirements in some situations. The chief premises of prototyping are that prototypes constitute a better means of communication than paper models, and that iteration is necessary to channel the inevitable learning process in the right direction.

AN APPROACH FOR REQUIREMENTS DEFINITION

The word 'prototyping' is sometimes used to refer to only a small part of the requirements definition phase (namely the part in which prototypes are realized and modified in an iterative cycle). In other cases, it is seen as a development approach which completely replaces the traditional way of developing information systems. However, we support yet another common interpretation of the term: in this book, it is seen as an alternative to the traditional way of defining requirements. Thus, prototyping is an approach for *requirements definition*, not a *development approach*.

We pointed out in the previous chapter that traditional methods and techniques still have a major role during prototyping (see also Section 3.7 and Part Two). The fact that prototypes are built has consequences for the way in which these methods and techniques are applied. In this book, the modified application of methods and techniques is regarded as being part of the prototyping process itself. Thus, when we use the word 'prototyping', we refer to the total process of requirements definition, with the combined use of prototypes and traditional methods and techniques, and not only to that part of the requirements definition phase in which prototypes are actually built and evaluated.

ITERATION

The basic premise of prototyping is that users cannot indicate what requirements and wishes they have for a system with no first-hand experience of it. Use of a prototype deepens both users' and information analysts' insight into the problem, and supports the learning process which the users must undergo. In the process, the prototype is modified in an iterative fashion until the requirements and wishes of the users with respect to the modelled aspect/subsystem are clear. Each successive prototype forms a closer approximation to the 'real' requirements. On the basis of the prototype, new requirements and wishes come to light, and it can be verified that the user and the developer have understood each other correctly.

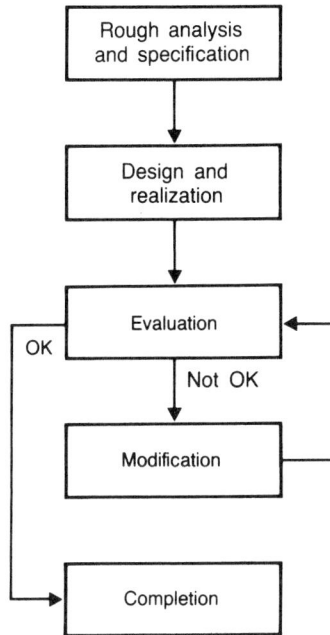

Figure 3.1 The requirements definition phase in the prototyping approach.

USER PARTICIPATION

Participation in the prototyping process makes considerable demands on the user's time. Although there is little empirical material on this subject, it may be assumed that participation in the prototyping process will take much more time than participation in a traditional requirements definition phase. In prototyping, the user is an active participant, evaluating prototypes, proposing improvements and, at the same time, continuing to obtain a deeper insight into his own requirements and wishes with respect to the information system. In the traditional approach to systems development, the user has a relatively passive role; the initiative always lies with the information analyst. Because the user has only a limited understanding of the language in which system requirements definitions are drawn up, he will not often become actively involved in the definition phase and its conclusion.

3.3 PROTOTYPING SUB-PHASES

In a requirements definition phase in which a prototyping approach is taken, five sub-phases can be distinguished (Fig. 3.1). In the first sub-phase ('rough analysis and specification') the problem is analyzed in global terms, with the aim of providing a solid basis for the subsequent sub-phases. In the second sub-phase ('design and

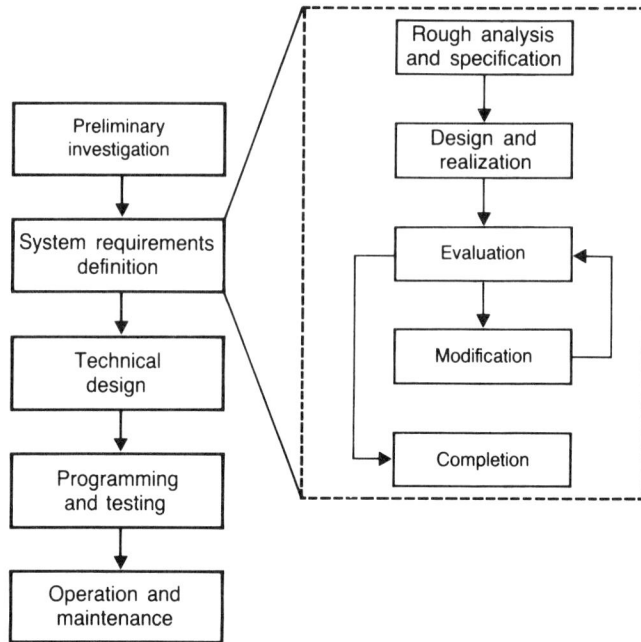

Figure 3.2 The place of prototyping in the development process.

realization') a prototype is built with the aid of advanced fourth-generation tools. In the third 'evaluation' sub-phase the prototype is handed over to the end-users and evaluated by them. If it becomes apparent that the specifications need adjustment then the necessary changes are made to the prototype in sub-phase four ('modification'). After this, the process returns to the preceding sub-phase. This cycle of evaluation and modification continues until uncertainty about the aspects modeled by the prototype has diminished to an acceptable level. In the final sub-phase ('completion') the system requirements definition is completed with performance and quality requirements.

The sub-phases of prototyping resemble those of the conventional linear process in many respects. There are, however, important differences: the prototyping process takes place within the requirements definition phase of the overall development process, and the individual sub-phases of prototyping are completed very quickly (and are not formally terminated). Prototyping creates a 'miniature life-cycle' within the requirements definition phase (Boar, 1984) (Fig. 3.2). The system resulting from the prototyping activity is, however, only a prototype. It must not be regarded as an operational information system, since it is generally far from complete and places particular emphasis on only a few aspects. Sometimes a prototype may be retained as the basis for construction of the production system. In other cases, the prototype is discarded and the subsequent design and realization of the production system are carried out in the traditional manner, but proceeding from a reliable and stable system requirements definition.

The realization of prototype systems, and their refinement in an iterative process, is only possible when powerful programming languages and tools are used. Examples are such fourth-generation languages as Software AG's Natural and ADR's Ideal, but languages such as LISP, Prolog and APL are also usable in this context. Without advanced tools, the construction of prototypes is too expensive and time consuming to be cost-effective. However, it is a mistake to think that the use of these Very High Level Languages (VHLLs), as they are sometimes called, necessarily equates with prototyping. Because they facilitate rapid system realization. VHLLs lend themselves pre-eminently to the iterative prototyping approach, but they can also be used effectively as a replacement for third-generation languages such as COBOL. Prototyping is primarily aimed at improving the *effectiveness* of the development process; VHLLs aim particularly at improving the *efficiency* of that process.

3.4 PROTOTYPING IN THE TECHNICAL DESIGN PHASE

It is often stated that prototyping can also play a role in the technical design phase. The aim is then to compare various technical designs for an information system so as to arrive at a system that satisfies the system requirements definition.

Once the system requirements definition has been established, it is, however, possible to work towards an end-product in a straight forward manner, certainly where application systems of an administrative or management character are concerned. General understanding of the technical design phase is continually improving and guidelines, rules and techniques are becoming available for this phase (consider, for example the 'coupling/binding' principles in software design, and access path analysis in database design). Designing an information system is becoming a science rather than an art; the need for the designer to construct prototypes is disappearing.

Sometimes, however, the system will be of such complexity that available design methods and techniques are inadequate. In such a situation, the designer can no longer arrive at a good technical design in a purely analytical way; a trial-and-error approach may be unavoidable. In our view, this should not be called prototyping. Although such an approach is characterized by both iteration and the use of prototypes, the third essential element of our definition of prototyping – user participation – is missing. Iteration is a characteristic of many development activities, which should not be called prototyping for that reason alone. Similarly, neither should every development strategy in which prototypes are employed.

During the technical design of very complex systems, mathematical models of the system can often play a useful role. Using simulation techniques, the designer can, for instance, determine what response times may be expected for a given system set-up. This is sometimes seen as a form of prototyping. However, the term 'simulation' is more appropriate here. In this book, we do not consider further the simulation of systems by the construction of formalized simulation models in a programming or simulation language.

3.5 CLASSES OF PROTOTYPING

Just as there are different kinds of prototype, there are different kinds of prototyping. In the literature one may find a number of classifications (see e.g. Cerveny *et al.* 1986; Floyd, 1984; Guimaraes, 1987; Law, 1985; Mayhew and Dearnly, 1987).

Firstly, classification may be based on the particular aspect which is modelled in a prototype. The kind of prototyping that concentrates on modelling the user interface of a system is generally called *user-interface prototyping*. If some real functionality is added to the prototype, the term *functional prototyping* is sometimes used. In this book we will also use these terms.

A second approach classifies prototyping according to the timing of the development process. Thus Floyd speaks of exploratory and experimental prototyping. *Exploratory prototyping* aims at discovering the user requirements, and is the kind of prototyping we refer to in this book. *Experimental prototyping* takes place in the technical design phase; its objective is to determine the adequacy of a proposed solution. Areas of concern may be the ability of the system to handle the anticipated workload (*performance prototyping*), or the selection of appropriate hardware (*hardware prototyping*).

In Section 3.4 we explained why we do not support the use of the term 'prototyping' to denote the trial-and-error approach sometimes necessary in the technical design phase. Since the kind of prototyping described in this book always takes place in the requirements definition phase, we have no use for a classification based on timing within the development process, and consequently do not use the terms 'exploratory' and 'experimental'.

A third kind of prototyping mentioned by Floyd (and many other authors) is *evolutionary prototyping*. In this development approach, the prototype evolves into the production system. Each version of the production system is then used as a prototype for its successor. However, this kind of prototyping should not really be bracketed together with exploratory and experimental prototyping. It does not refer to the phase in which a prototyping approach is followed, but to the use made of the prototype after the prototyping activity has come to an end. This criterion is the basis for yet another classification of approaches to prototyping found in literature. If a prototype is used as the basis for the production system one speaks of *keep-it* or, as mentioned above, *evolutionary prototyping*; if the prototype is thrown away the term *throw-away prototyping* is generally used.

However, we do not favor these last two terms. What happens to a prototype after conclusion of the prototyping activity has little to do with the prototyping activity itself. Furthermore, the term 'evolutionary prototyping' implies that prototyping is seen as a strategy for developing systems, instead of for obtaining requirements. In Section 3.8 we explain why a clear distinction should be made between evolutionary development and prototyping.

3.6 STRATEGIES, METHODS, TECHNIQUES AND TOOLS

We have defined prototyping as an 'approach' to establishing requirements definitions. Prototyping is often, perhaps loosely, referred to as a 'method' or a 'technique'. This is unfortunate, because each of these terms has acquired distinct meaning in the field of information systems engineering, and neither is correctly applicable to prototyping. The terms 'method' and 'technique' are not infrequently interchanged both with one another and with related terms such as 'methodology' and 'tool'. To substantiate our definition of prototyping, it is necessary to examine carefully the term 'approach' and its putative rivals in this field – method, technique, methodology and tool.

APPROACH

An approach (or strategy) defines the broad characteristics of the development process, such as the guiding principles to be followed and the chief intermediate goals, while leaving the detailed course of action to be determined at a different level or time. In the context of information systems development, strategic decisions at the project level will concern such matters as:

1. In-house development or purchase of a package.
2. Development by end-users, or by professional systems developers.
3. The degree of user participation in the development process.
4. The choice of a data-oriented or a process-oriented approach.

The choice of prototyping for the requirements definition phase determines the principles (such as user involvement and iteration) and the intermediate goals (the sub-phases illustrated in Fig. 3.2), leaving further details to be decided at a later date.

METHOD

In information systems development, the term 'method' is generally used specifically to mean a prescribed course of action and a set of standards for dealing with a specific aspect or part of the development process. Typically a method also defines the documentation to be produced in each step (the 'deliverables'). It specifies in detail the activities to be carried out to achieve a given objective, in contrast to a strategy which gives only the general characteristics of the process. Another important feature that distinguishes methods from strategies is their often proprietary character. The well-known methods are copyright property, and are promoted or marketed under trade names, either as separate products or as part of a 'methodology' (see below).

Methods can be divided into two main classes: *project management methods* (such as Method/1 of Arthur Andersen or SDM of the Dutch firm Pandata (Hice *et al.*, 1987)) for controlling information system development projects, and *development methods* (such as Yourdon's Structured Design) for executing such projects. In this book, the term 'method' refers only to development methods unless otherwise stated.

TECHNIQUE

A method generally specifies one or more techniques to be used when performing specific tasks. A method addresses the 'what to do' aspects of system development, while a technique addresses the 'how to do it'. In common with methods, techniques may apply either to project management and control (e.g. PERT) or to project execution (e.g. Dataflow Diagramming). In contrast to methods, most techniques are non-proprietary and become available through academic channels. Typically, a method may incorporate a number of techniques, and a given technique may be used in a wide variety of competing proprietary methods.

METHODOLOGY

A method, as defined above, generally addresses a specific phase or aspect of the development process. In practice it is necessary to combine several methods to provide complete coverage. For methods to combine efficiently and effectively, they must not overlap and must have well-defined interfaces. Some such comprehensive sets of methods are marketed as proprietary products; James Martin's Information Engineering is an example. The generic term for such products is 'methodology'.

For an integrated set of distinct methods to earn the designation 'methodology' it should embody, or at least embrace, a definite theory or philosophy for solving the problems of developing information systems. In practice, the philosophy behind the methodology is not always explicit or even identifiable, and in a few cases the logic which unites the components appears to be no more than the 'logic' of marketing requirements. However, for want of a better term, we shall continue to use 'methodology' as a generic term for proprietary multiple-method combinations which cover (or aim to cover) the whole development process. Since prototyping is not linked to specific proprietary methods and has no ambitions beyond the requirements definition phase, it would be misleading to describe it as a methodology.

TOOL

In the context of systems development, and in this book, the term 'tool' refers exclusively to computer software for providing assistance with various tasks. A tool may vary from something limited in scope, such as a drawing program, to a comprehensive set of software such as an analyst workbench or a fourth-generation development environment. There are proprietary tools to support specific techniques, and tools to aid in the execution of specific methods. Many proprietary methods are sold together with a set of tools; some tools are useful in connection with a variety of methods or techniques. Although there is little risk of confusing prototyping with a tool in this sense, it is important to maintain a clear distinction between methods, techniques and the tools that support them.

3.7 PROTOTYPING VERSUS STRUCTURED METHODS

Although prototyping is neither a method nor a technique, it is in no sense in conflict with structured methods and techniques. As will be apparent from the foregoing discussion, these terms relate to different aspects of the development processes. We shall enlarge on this in the following paragraphs.

PROTOTYPES MODEL ANOTHER ASPECT OF A SYSTEM

Different aspects of the system demand different modeling 'languages'. Top-down graphical modeling techniques such as dataflow diagramming are principally suited to the modeling of functions which the system must fulfil. For the modeling of the information structure, for example, the entity-relationship diagrams of Chen or Merise might be used. However, graphical notation is inadequate when the often complex rules applicable to an information structure have to be recorded; for that purpose a (semi-)formal language is more suitable.

Prototypes are first and foremost effective ways of modeling a user interface. This is not to imply that the external appearance of the system is all that may be learned from a prototype. Through the development of prototypes a deeper insight is generally obtained into the problem and the overall requirements of the system intended to solve it.[1] However, for modeling and documenting the problem area, and such things as the system and database structure, traditional diagramming techniques are more suitable than prototypes. Moreover, traditional methods offer much more support to the analysis process. The top-down approach that characterizes many process-oriented development methods makes it possible to divide a complex problem into manageable pieces. For the modeling of a data structure, prototypes offer little support. It makes sense to develop prototypes only after sufficient insight has been gained into the problem, and after a broad outline of an information system to solve that problem has been made, using traditional methods and techniques.

Prototypes primarily model different aspects of systems than the traditional methods and techniques. They therefore constitute an addition to the arsenal of aids available to the information analyst in the requirements definition phase, and must not be considered as a substitute for them. During a requirements definition phase in which a prototyping approach is taken, the traditional methods and techniques function as *analysis* and *documentation* aids for modeling the data structure and functions which the system is intended to support. For modeling the user-interface, and as a means of *communication* between developers and the future users of the system, prototypes are deployed. The superiority of prototypes as a communication medium over the paper-based models used until now has been explained in the previous chapter.

PROTOTYPES ARE SYSTEMS TOO

Although prototypes typically model only aspects and parts of a system, they are still systems: they have to be analyzed, designed and realized. Furthermore, in view of the iterative nature of the prototyping process, prototypes must be as flexible and understandable as 'real' systems, and perhaps even more so. Finally, if we want to capitalize on the prototyping effort by re-using parts of a prototype as the basis for the production system, these parts need to be of a high quality. This necessitates a disciplined and structured development of prototypes (Riddle, 1984).

So, prototyping clearly must not be equated with the unstructured way of working usually employed before the arrival of structured methods and techniques. Unfortunately, this is how it is sometimes interpreted. It is often stated that the prototyping approach is 'nothing new' – that it is the way things have always been done. Prototyping sometimes becomes an alibi for the 'doers' among the system developers who (with some relief) set aside the structured analysis methods and immediately start to write programs, just as in the 'good old days'. In such situations, the anxiety that prototyping leads to an unstructured, untestable and unmaintainable information system is justified. Prototyping must take place in a structured manner so that both the process and its results can be controlled.

3.8 RELATED TERMS

The term 'prototyping' is often confused with some more or less related concepts. This severely hinders a proper evaluation of the prototyping approach, since invalid arguments about its merits and demerits enter the discussion on the basis of such errors of association.

EVOLUTIONARY DEVELOPMENT
A good example of a concept related to, but clearly distinct from, prototyping is 'evolutionary development'. In this approach, emphasis is placed on achieving a flexible and expandable production system (Land, 1982), so that when the requirements change a modified version of the system can be realized very quickly. A similar situation is sometimes encountered in prototyping when a new prototype is produced to meet changes in users' requirements. The essential difference between evolutionary development and prototyping is that in the former the aim is a quick realization of successive versions of the production system itself, while prototypes of (parts of) the system are involved in the latter. This distinction is definitely of more than academic interest – after all, a prototype and a production system have to meet completely different requirements (for example, in respect of reliability, performance or completeness). The two strategies have different objectives, and this is reflected in various ways during development. Prototyping and evolutionary development cannot, therefore (as is sometimes suggested in the literature) be very well used in combination. There is no reason why they should be combined, since each strategy is aimed at a totally different problem situation. Prototyping assumes that 'real' requirements exist. To establish just what the user actually needs it may be necessary to go through a number of iterations, but ultimately the requirements definition will stabilize. The basic assumption of evolutionary development, on the other hand, is that the requirements will be subject to continual change. In such a situation there is no point in prototyping, because the iterative process will never end.

Failure to draw a proper distinction between prototyping and evolutionary development can lead to the wrong conclusion. It is sometimes stated that an environment subject to rapid change demands a prototyping approach (see Kauber (1985) for example). It is clear that this conclusion is invalid; such an environment demands a flexible end-product – in other words an evolutionary development approach.

INCREMENTAL DEVELOPMENT

A concept closely related to the evolutionary development approach, and frequently confused with it, is 'incremental development'. In the incremental development approach, system development is started with the intention of delivering an initial version of the system to satisfy a sub-set of the specified requirements. Later versions provide for the remaining requirements. This approach achieves user profit from early availability of a system that, though still incomplete, is at least usable and satisfies some of the principal information needs. This is an effective answer to the often-voiced complaint that too much time elapses between the completion of the system requirements definition and the installation of the required system.

The successive versions of a system developed in both evolutionary and incremental development clearly differ in character. In evolutionary development, a new version of the whole system is developed each time. In the case of incremental development, the system as a whole is built up step by step, and each successive version consists of the previous version unchanged plus a number of new functions. Obviously, this is an idealization; in practice the two approaches may not be strictly distinguishable. For instance, in an evolutionary approach a new version of the system will sometimes include new functions. Nevertheless, it is useful to maintain a distinction between evolutionary and incremental development, since these two development strategies have different aims and will necessitate different compositions of the project and the product.

It is, of course, possible to develop a system incrementally and at the same time to follow an evolutionary approach for developing particular components of the system. Similarly, incremental development combines well with prototyping. Consideration must be given to what is the best development approach for each component to be developed in a system, in the light of the characteristics of the problem situation.

PARTICIPATIVE DEVELOPMENT

Another development approach regularly confused with prototyping is 'participative development' (see Hirschheim, (1983) for example). This is an approach in which there is a high degree of user involvement in the development process. The fact that the prototyping process is characterized by an active role for users does not infer that every development approach which emphasizes user participation is identical to prototyping. Only when user participation is coupled with both a high level of iteration and an extensive utilization of prototypes is the term prototyping justified.

END-USER COMPUTING

A popular misconception is that the development of applications by end-users (end-user computing) and prototyping are similar. Again, the two approaches are unconnected: a statement is made in the one case about the person or group which carries out the development, and in the other about the way in which the development is carried out. Of course, a user with suitable expertise can also realize applications using a prototyping-like approach, but the average end-user will not have the skills necessary for prototyping; the structured approach described in this book is particularly intended for information analysts. To prevent blurring of the terminology, it is advisable to use only the term 'end-user computing', and not 'prototyping', to refer to the development of (small and simple) applications by end-users themselves.

SYNONYMS

Finally, a comment on some synonyms for the term 'prototyping' is appropriate. Synonyms or near-synonyms include 'heuristic development' (Berrisford and Wetherbe, 1979) and 'adaptive design' (Alavi, 1984b). These terms are not generally defined unambiguously. In some cases the authors wish to indicate by the use of such a term that there are minor distinctions between the approach they describe and their interpretation of prototyping; however, the essence of the various development approaches remains identical.

3.9 PROTOTYPING AND THE THREE-LEVEL APPROACH

The ISO three-level approach to information systems (briefly described in the Appendix) gives the information system developer a general model for conceptualizing information systems. This approach distinguishes three aspects or 'levels' of an information system: the information level, the data level and the internal level. This provides the developer with a means of studying various aspects of the information system under development independently of one another, so that the complexity of the development task is reduced.

The three-level principle, and especially the stringent distinction between the conceptual and external level which it introduces, has a significant influence on the process of defining system requirements. Consequently, it has a concrete effect on the course of the prototyping process and on the rough analysis and specification sub-phase within prototyping. In this section, we make some remarks about the relationship between this analytical framework and prototyping.

To understand this relationship, let us first define exactly what we mean by '(system) requirements definition'. A requirements definition should incorporate all the requirements that the user lays down for the information system to be developed. It should always include a complete *conceptual* description of the system, which lists the information it must be able to store and the functions that operate on that information. Since the arrival of interactive systems, the user generally also specifies requirements for the *external* form of the system. In these cases, the requirements definition should include a description of the user interface (screen and report layouts, and dialogue structure). The system requirements definition may also contain requirements for the *internal* realization of the system (for example the type of computer, or the maximum size of the program). Finally, performance and quality requirements are also part of the system requirements definition. These include user's needs in respect of response times, security and reliability.

Prototyping is primarily aimed at obtaining a clearer understanding about what the user requires of the outer layer of the system – the user interface. Prototypes are the best medium for modeling this aspect of an information system. Since there is a direct relationship between the external, conceptual and internal levels, prototypes can also be used as a way of deepening understanding of the conceptual and the internal aspects. With prototyping, users and developers can communicate on the basis of a concrete model that is comprehensible to both. By discussing the user interface, the developer can learn a great deal about the way the user sees the world, and about the patterns that prevail in it.

To take an example: when a user indicates that an item of data must appear in a particular format at a particular place on the screen, the developer has learned something not only about the user interface, but also about the need of the user for that data item. A second example: when a user reports that a particular combination of data values is not allowed, the developer can add a constraint (or rule) to the conceptual schema. In both examples, the prototype functions as a means of verifying that the conceptual schema (as embodied in, for instance, an entity-relationship diagram) is complete and correct. It is even possible to learn something about performance requirements on the basis of a prototype. After using the prototype, the user will raise requirements concerning reliability, response time, security, etc. However, this is really a by-product of the prototyping process; the identification of performance requirements is not the primary aim of prototyping.

In general, during the early iterations of the prototyping process the developer will ask the user to concentrate on conceptual aspects (the completeness and correctness of the prototype), and provisionally to pay no attention to the form in which the system is cast. For example, the user is asked if everything he wants to know about a particular thing (e.g. an order) is present on a screen. At this stage, the gross errors and omissions will come to light. The form of the system (dialogues, screen and report layouts, data formats) is dealt with thoroughly in later iterations. The changes to the system can then remain relatively small.

Because prototypes model the user interface there is a danger that conceptual aspects will be neglected in a project using prototyping. In this case the developer must be aware that he is concentrating on external aspects, and must not forget that other aspects also require attention. It has already been emphasized that prototyping does not make traditional methods superfluous.

NOTE

1. Sèe also the examples in Section 3.9.

Chapter 4

Choosing the Right Development Approach

The present decade is marked by very rapid and radical developments in the field of information technology. New aids for developing information systems are proliferating, with direct consequences for the way information problems are, and must be, solved. The large number of system development strategies, structured development methods and software tools currently available makes it essential that a well-founded choice is made of the way in which the information problem is going to be solved.

In practice, not enough recognition is given to the fact that there are various options open for reaching a solution to an information problem, and that a well-considered choice of these options can substantially increase the chance of the development project being successful. In general, the information systems department sticks to one development methodology. When this fails to generate the desired result (a timely, efficiently produced solution to the information problem), the blame is all too often placed on the strategy and methods used. However, it can often be established that the cause is not so much to be sought in the poor quality of the methodology, as in the fact that the development strategy or method used was unsuitable for the problem in hand. Development strategies and methods are rarely inherently either good or bad; rather, they can be described as being more – or less – suitable to a particular context (Iivari, 1984).

4.1 A CONTINGENCY APPROACH

When an information problem arises, the first thing that has to be determined is who can best solve the problem: the end-user or the information systems department. In some cases the end-user, aided by advanced, very user-friendly tools, can develop an application autonomously. In many other cases it is impossible or inadvisable for the user to do his own system development, so the information systems department must enter the fray. After all, members of that department are specially trained in, and organized for, the development of large, complex and high-quality information systems, and are capable of seeing such systems in a broader context.

For the efficient and effective development of information systems, these professional systems developers now have access to a gamut of strategies, methods, techniques and software tools. These can be broadly classified into: management aids supporting project management in planning and controlling a project, and development aids supporting application system developers (see Chapter 3). In the initiation phase of a project, the project leader has to choose both the project model (the phase structure for the required activities) and the development approach, methods, techniques and tools to be used. The choice is contingent on the characteristics of the information problem and its context. Of course, it is not necessary for the whole information system to be developed using the same development aids; the chosen 'cocktail' may be different for different sub-systems.

There are few concrete guidelines yet available to project leaders to aid them in selecting the right development strategy. In the sparse literature on this subject, an article by Shomenta *et al.* (1983) takes a fairly prominent place. This describes a procedure whereby it is possible to arrive at a choice of one of three development strategies: development by end-users on a personal computer, development by end-users with the aid of a fourth-generation language on the mainframe and development by the information systems department. This choice is based on 18 concrete characteristics of the information system to be developed – such as the number of simultaneous users, the number of locations where the system will be used and the number of persons with an interest in the stored data. In other publications on this subject yet other development strategies are distinguished (see, for example: Ahituv *et al.*, 1984; Flint *et al.*, 1983; Santos, 1986; Schonberger, 1980). Further, there have been publications on specific topics in this area. For instance, both Davis (1982) and Naumann *et al.* (1980) discuss which strategy for determining information needs is best in a given problem situation.

Just as for development strategies, there is not simply one best approach to project management. A project manager must make a choice from the means available to him for planning and controlling a project, on the basis of the project's characteristics. McFarlan and McKenney (1983) give a few guidelines in this area. They propose that the choice must depend on the project risk: the chance that a project will overrun its budget or schedule, that the system will be unsatisfactory, or even that the entire project will be an utter failure. This project risk is determined by the relative size of the project, the amount of experience with the technology adopted, and the 'project structure' (the structuredness of the problem). McFarlan and McKenney describe a practical procedure on the basis of which the total risk can be estimated in a given situation.

It must be concluded, however, that the definitive publication on the subject has not yet seen the light of day. Work is being done on several fronts to draw up concrete guidelines for selecting the most suitable strategy, methods and software tools in a given problem situation. It is reasonable to expect that within the foreseeable future a more systematic approach to this problem of choice will emerge. Until then the project leader will largely have to trust to his experience and common sense.

PROTOTYPING VERSUS THE TRADITIONAL APPROACH

One approach to the requirements definition phase is prototyping. The prototyping concept appears to be attractive to both users and system developers. There may be a dangerous tendency to take this approach every time a new information problem arises, without due consideration of its advantages and disadvantages. Prototyping is no panacea; there are many situations in which it is ineffective, unwise or just impossible to use. In the project initiation phase it must be considered if it makes sense to combine the use of conventional diagramming techniques and the development of prototypes. The project leader will have to determine the best approach to achieve a complete, accurate and stable requirements definition in the particular situation.

Prototyping may be restricted to modelling the user interface. In the previous chapter we noted that the conventional methods pay little or no attention to modelling this aspect. In other words, if a prototype user interface is not developed, one aspect of the system is, in fact ignored. With the help of contemporary tools such as screen painters, a user interface can be created and modified more quickly than if it were modelled on paper. Therefore, user-interface prototyping is practically always to be recommended – unless, of course, the user interface is unimportant to the application under development, or users have no opinions about it or no say in the form the system will eventually take. To prototype or not is far less clear when functional prototyping is considered. Functional prototypes illustrate the same aspects of the system as models made using conventional diagramming techniques, and developing such prototypes can be costly.

The remainder of this chapter describes the criteria on which to base the choice between functional prototyping and a conventional approach to requirements definition. In Section 4.2, prototyping is examined from a cost/benefit point of view. On the basis of this section, it is possible to determine whether prototyping is *desirable* in a give problem situation. Section 4.3 describes the situations in which prototyping is *possible*. Finally, Section 4.4 contains a summary.

4.2 THE COST-EFFECTIVENESS OF PROTOTYPING

The decision to use prototyping in a particular situation has to be justified from an economic standpoint; the expected benefits should be greater than the expected costs. However, neither costs nor benefits are easily quantified. To obtain valid numeric data it would be necessary to measure the development costs of a large number of systems, both developed in the traditional way and developed using prototyping. Subsequently the resulting systems would have to be used under controlled conditions, with statistical methods being employed to filter out any 'noise'. The relative costs or benefits of prototyping would then follow from a comparison of the life-cycle costs in the respective categories. Such an experimental set-up would be expensive and very time consuming, and would have to extend over an extremely long period. Consequently there is still almost a complete lack of empirical data of this kind. The results of the few studies that have been made in this area are virtually impossible to compare because the term 'prototyping' is interpreted differently in each case (compare for example Boehm *et al.* (1984) and Alavi (1984a)).

The cost of software development depends not only on the strategy adopted but also on a large number of other factors. Efforts to improve knowledge in this area are progressing with some difficulty. This is illustrated by the fact that no one has yet found a satisfactory technique for estimating the costs of development – preferably one which can be applied early in the project. Boehm's (1981) standard work in this field – *Software Engineering Economics* – describes a model embodying 15 distinct factors which should jointly determine the cost of software development. In a more recent publication Jones (1986) has as many as 45 such factors. Experience with models for estimating software development costs has so far produced little in the way of positive results. Such models invariably fail to take all the cost-determining factors (*cost drivers*) into account, so that estimates prove to have little accuracy.

What the research in this field has confirmed is the belief, long cherished in practice, that the cost of software development depends heavily on the quality of the developers – it is not so much the method that matters but the person who applies it. It also appears that the use of a more advanced language has a significant influence on development costs. It must be borne in mind that investigations which try to compare the costs of prototyping with the costs of the conventional approach are attempting to reduce or neutralize the influence of other – perhaps more important – cost drivers. So instead of determining which measures produce the largest rise in productivity, research of this kind aims to establish the effect of prototyping on the productivity of the system development function. The analysis below should be seen in this perspective.

Given the present understanding of the cost/benefit effects of prototyping, it is still too early even to attempt to pronounce the last word on the economy of prototyping. The following analysis is thus largely tentative and qualitative in character. Section 4.2.1 describes the reduction in life-cycle costs that may be expected from prototyping. Section 4.2.2 deals with cost increases entailed by prototyping. Section 4.2.3 gives a comparative summary of the costs and benefits. Finally, Section 4.2.4 describes a few of the benefits of prototyping which cannot easily be translated into financial terms, but which are none the less very real.

4.2.1 Benefits of prototyping

The *benefits* of the prototyping approach are, primarily, reduction of *uncertainty* about the nature of the information problem and the requirements that users lay down for a solution to that problem. 'Uncertainty' is the difference between the knowledge already possessed about a problem and that which is needed about it to arrive at an acceptable solution. Conventional techniques also aim at eliminating this uncertainty, but are not always, as previously discussed, sufficiently successful. This section deals first with the savings that result from the reduction of uncertainty, and then with other benefits of prototyping.

REDUCTION OF MAINTENANCE COSTS

There is a direct relationship between uncertainty about an information problem and the likely maintenance costs of the information system intended to solve it. Reducing uncertainty leads to a fall in maintenance costs. The considerable savings resulting from this have been illustrated in Chapter 2, where it was shown that as much as 50 per cent of the total life-cycle costs of an information system may be directly caused by the poor quality of the requirements definition. In a typical case the use of

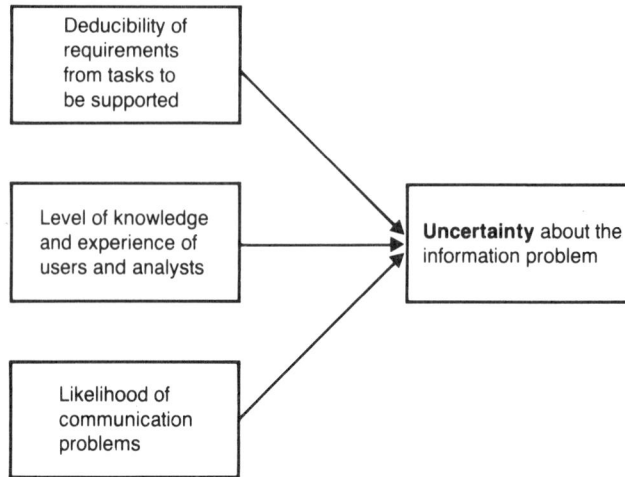

Figure 4.1 Uncertainty-determining factors.

prototyping will thus bring substantial savings. However, when there is no uncertainty about the users' requirements and wishes, the benefits of this approach for requirements definition are negligible. In this situation, the conventional approach and prototyping will result in the same (low) maintenance costs. To assess the potential benefits from prototyping in a particular situation, it must be established what degree of uncertainty exists.

Uncertainty can relate to conceptual as well as external aspects of the system. In particular, uncertainty about the conceptual level can have very serious consequences. In such a case, there will be lack of clarity about the system's functions and about the structure of the database. Errors and omissions in this area generally necessitate radical and expensive modifications. Uncertainty about the form the system must take has less serious financial consequences, but may have a serious effect on user satisfaction. Lack of clarity in this area leads to a less user-friendly system, but one which still does what is required. Modifying the user interface is less radical than making functional changes to the system. On the basis of the criteria given below (see Fig. 4.1) it is possible to check whether, in a given situation, uncertainty exists at the conceptual level.

(a) Deducibility of requirements from tasks to be supported. In some cases, the requirements for an information system follow from analysis of the tasks to be supported. The problem situation then has the following features:

1. The processes which the new system must support are well defined. This is directly related to the routine and/or repetitive character of the task (Mann and Watson, 1984).
2. The part of the organization which is to be supported is stable in its structure and its operation (Davis, 1982).

When the requirements for the information system can be established by analysis of the part of the organization to be supported – in other words, when they follow directly from the tasks to be supported – there is little risk of a serious degree of uncertainty. In such cases, communication problems between developers and users are unlikely, and the system's specifications will be fairly stable.

(b) Level of knowledge and experience of users and analysts.   When the requirements definition of the new system does not follow entirely from the tasks to be supported, it is necessary to rely on the insight of the system's future users and of the information analysts involved in developing the system. The better the understanding of those involved in the problem situation, the greater is the chance that the 'real' information problem will be identified, and the less the likelihood that the requirements definition will undergo changes after users have had experience of using the system.

The users' and information analysts' insights into the information problem and its required solution depend in particular on the following:

1. Knowledge and experience in the relevant application area.
2. Previous experience with similar information systems.
3. Experience with automated information systems in general.
4. The stability of the part of the organization to be supported.
5. The complexity of the system to be developed.

When neither users nor information analysts have a sufficient understanding of the problem situation, prototyping is the only correct approach. However, when at least one of the parties has sufficient insight into the problem situation and into the requirements of the system to be developed, the need to use models to support a learning process is absent. The information problem is known, so there is little risk that the system requirements definition will change as a result of users gaining experience in using the system. In such cases prototypes may still play a useful role as a means of communication (see c).

(c) Likelihood of communication problems.   When users and information analysts need to communicate intensively with each other, uncertainty about the information needs can result from the two parties failing to speak the same language. In this case, uncertainty is caused not by a lack of understanding of the information problem, but by a poor capacity to communicate that understanding. The risk of communication problems is high when:

1. Users have no experience of the analysis language being used.
2. Users have a negative attitude towards the language used by the information analysts.
3. Users are not able to cope with a language that assumes a capacity for abstract thinking.
4. Information analysts lack experience of the relevant application area and the language of that area.

The greatest risk of uncertainty at the conceptual level occurs when the system requirements do not follow from a task analysis, neither users nor information analysts have knowledge or experience in the application area and there is a high risk of communication problems. In such circumstances prototyping will almost certainly lead to considerable savings.

OTHER BENEFITS

Besides cutting maintenance costs by reducing uncertainty, there are further savings to be gained by using prototyping. Compared with a conventional linear project, the (functional) testing phase will be shorter and less expensive. (This is, by the way, not because the costs of this phase disappear when prototyping is used, but because they are largely shifted to the requirements definition phase.) Prototyping gives further benefits because the introduction of the new system into the organization progresses more smoothly. In the first place, the system will generally be better adapted to the organization and, in the second place, users involved in the prototyping activity will already be familiar with the system. In many cases the training costs will turn out to be significantly lower (again, because they are largely shifted to the requirements definition phase).

When a prototype can be used as the basis for (part of) the production system there are considerable savings in the design and realization phases, in addition to the reduction in maintenance costs. In this case, an important part of the information system is already available after prototyping. This situation occurs particularly when the prototype has been built using the same language and in the same (technical) environment as will be used for the production system. Many fourth-generation development environments offer excellent facilities for the realization of both prototypes and production systems.

Difficult to quantify, but just as real, are the savings resulting from the avoidance of *opportunity* costs. The users will have a fully effective system at their disposal at an earlier point in time. This can result in considerable savings. For instance, earlier availability of an effective logistic system brings forward the achievement of savings in inventory costs. Reduced project throughput times and increased flexibility of the organization are manifested in competitive edge for the company. The extent to which the company really obtains an advantage over its competitors depends strongly on the speed with which benefits are realized – after all, the competition will not be standing still. It is possible to think of many examples where the time of completion of an information system will be critical to the gaining of competitive advantage by the enterprise.

4.2.2 Costs of prototyping

It will be clear that the costs of prototyping depend heavily on the quality and the advanced capabilities of the tools that are used. When the user interface is created with a screen painter and report writer, the costs will be many times lower than if conventional development aids had been used. The use of powerful procedural and non-procedural languages as part of an integrated development environment reduces both development and modification costs of a prototype. When a good relational (or semi-relational) database system is available, modification of the database structure and reorganization of the database are fairly simple and cheap to perform. Restructuring a network database is many times more expensive, and if only a hierarchical database management system (DBMS) is available it is wise to think at least twice before taking this step! A hierarchical DBMS is far more appropriate to a development project in which the database structure can be specified accurately and rigorously without the help of prototyping.

The cost of prototyping will further depend on the number of iterations needed to arrive at an acceptable prototype. The number of iterations is related to the degree of uncertainty about the system requirements at the start of the prototyping process. With good tools and a well-constructed prototype, the cost of making changes will remain low.

Even when advanced tools are available, the costs associated with prototyping will be higher than those of a conventional analysis. When the level of uncertainty is very high, the traditional methods will result in a set of requirements in which uncertainty remains. When prototyping is applied in a similar situation, the work that must be done is the same as in a conventional project. However, in this case it is also necessary to develop (and have users evaluate) one or more prototypes of aspects or parts of the system, in order to reduce the uncertainty to an acceptable level.

4.2.3 Cost/benefit evaluation

The savings resulting from the use of prototyping are realized mainly during the maintenance phase, and to a lesser degree – when the prototype can function as a basis for the production system – during the design and realization phases. Spectacular savings occur only when there is uncertainty about the information problem and its solution. The extra costs of the prototyping approach occur in the requirements definition phase. Prototyping thus leads to a new cost pattern. This is shown in Fig. 4.2. To avoid confusing the effects of prototyping with those of using fourth-generation languages, five scenarios are distinguished in this figure:

(a) A conventional approach during the requirements definition phase, and realization of the production system in a third-generation language.
(b) Prototyping during the requirements definition phase, and realization of the production system in a third-generation language (the prototype being discarded at the end of the prototyping activity).
(c) A conventional approach during the requirements definition phase, and realization of the production system in a fourth-generation language.
(d) Prototyping during the requirements definition phase, and realization of the production system in a fourth-generation language (the prototype being discarded at the end of the prototyping activity).
(e) Prototyping during the requirements definition phase, and the prototype functioning as the basis for the production system.

To obtain a correct view of the effects of prototyping, scenario 'a' should be compared

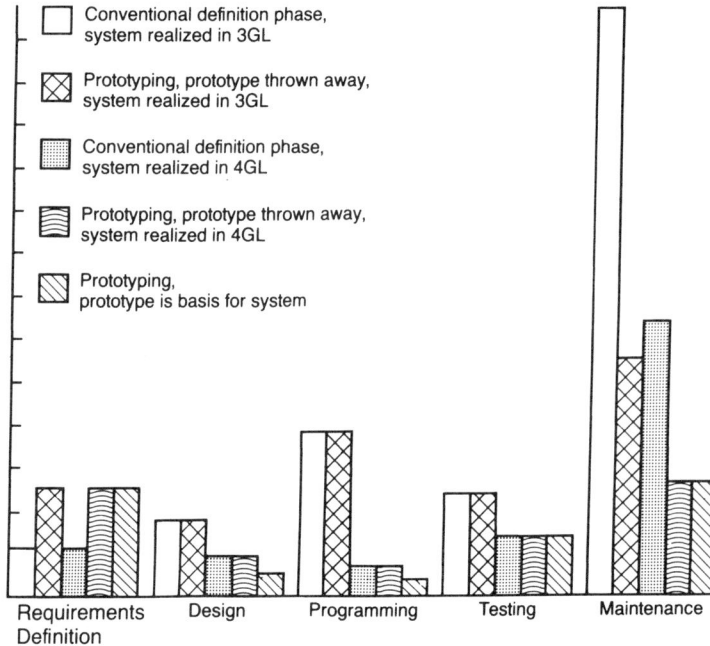

Figure 4.2 Expected changed cost pattern resulting from the use of prototyping and fourth-generation languages.

with 'b', scenario 'c' with 'd', and scenario 'd' with 'e'. The changed cost patterns resulting from use of a fourth-generation language become apparent from comparing scenario 'a' with 'c', and scenario 'b' with 'd'. Figure 4.2 illustrates how the greatest savings occur when prototyping is applied and the prototype is retained as the basis for the production system (scenario 'e') instead of a conventional development in a third-generation language (scenario 'a'). These savings, however, are not entirely due to the use of prototyping; they are partly the result of using fourth-generation tools. In practice, there is often no distinction made between the effects of prototyping and those of fourth-generation tools. This should be apparent from an investigation by Längle *et al.* (1984), in which a large number of organizations were asked why they used (or intended to use) prototyping. The most usual answer given to this question is 'shorter development time', which is a result of using powerful development tools, and certainly not of prototyping.

In interpreting Fig. 4.2, the reader should bear in mind that it gives only an indication. No absolute significance should be attached to the heights of the histogram bars. The figure is based on a number of assumptions, which are supported only partially by empirical data. Any changes to these assumptions will of course lead to a changed figure. The assumptions are:

1. Sixty per cent of the total life-cycle costs of an information system are maintenance costs (costs occurring after delivery of the system). This figure comes from an early study by IBM.

2. When a fourth-generation language is used, but analysis and design are carried out in the traditional way (scenario 'c'), the maintenance costs are still 60 per cent of the life-cycle costs. There is no reason to suppose that this should be any less since the system requirements definition will be of the same quality.

3. The distribution of costs over the various development phases in the conventional project process (scenario 'a') comes from Zelkowitz *et al.* (1979). However, these figures differ from one researcher to another because each uses his own definition of the phases, and the cost pattern depends strongly on the type and size of the information system (Boehm, 1981).

4. The savings that occur as a result of using a fourth-generation language have been investigated by Rudolph (1983). The savings indicated in the figure (scenario 'c' compared with 'a', and scenario 'd' compared with 'b') appear conservative when compared with Rudolph's findings.

5. If there is great uncertainty about the requirements definition, several prototypes must be developed to remove this uncertainty. The costs of these exceed the cost of the design and realization of a production system in a fourth-generation language.

6. Sixty per cent of the total maintenance costs are caused by poor system requirements definitions (IBM). Through prototyping, these costs can be completely avoided. This assumes that after prototyping the system requirements definition forms a complete representation of the end-users' requirements and wishes, and that even long-term use of the information system leads to no significant changes in the information needs.

When an economic evaluation of prototyping in the context of a particular problem situation is required, it must first be decided whether the prototype will be used as the basis of the production system, or whether it will be discarded. If the former, prototyping is almost always to be recommended. In those situations where there is no uncertainty, prototyping is then simply another way of constructing the production system. The extra costs in the requirements definition phase are recouped by lower costs in the design and realization phases. The number of iterations in the requirements definition phase in such cases remains low. When there is uncertainty about the information problem, prototyping reduces that uncertainty and thereby leads to considerable savings in the maintenance phase. Against this must be weighed the increase in cost of the requirements definition phase, which might require many iterations.

However, at that stage the information system can still be modified fairly easily. Making changes during the maintenance phase is many times more expensive (even when the system is realized in a fourth-generation environment). This is because an operational system must satisfy all the requirements, including performance and security. Measures taken to satisfy such requirements increase the system's complexity and hence reduce its flexibility. In contrast, a prototype is generally incomplete, many constraints can be ignored, and the prototype is less complex and easier to modify than a production system. Another cause of high cost involved in changing a production system is the fact that such a system is already entrenched in the organization. Modification of a system after delivery often means that organizational procedures must be changed.

When a prototype is discarded after conclusion of the prototyping activity, more attention has to be paid to the cost/benefit question. Since, in this case, the increased cost of the requirements definition phase is not balanced by savings in the design and realization phases, the extra cost of prototyping should not exceed the anticipated reduction in maintenance costs. When the degree of uncertainty about the information problem is great, a prototyping approach is generally justified, in view of the considerable savings to be expected in maintenance costs. If there is no uncertainty, it is unnecessary and inadvisable to follow a prototyping approach. The increased costs in the requirements definition phase are then not made up for by reduced maintenance costs.

Thus, unless the prototype can form the basis of the production system, it is advisable – from the standpoint of the 'hard' costs and benefits – to use the prototyping approach only when there is substantial uncertainty about the requirements. However, there can be other motives for wishing to follow a prototyping approach. These are discussed in the next section.

4.2.4 Intangible benefits

In addition to the material benefits of prototyping described above, the use of this approach for requirements definition has several further positive effects which are particularly difficult – or even impossible – to quantify. These intangible benefits must, of course, also be taken into account during the selection of a requirements definition approach.

USER ATTITUDE

In many publications about prototyping, mention is made of the positive influence this approach appears to have in practice on the attitude of end-users toward both the development process and the information systems department. This positive change in attitude is principally a consequence of the active involvement of the user in the prototyping process, and the improved communications between system developers and end-users.

The high level of participation makes it possible for users to influence strongly both the course of the development process and its outcome. The users largely determine what form the information system must take and what functionality it must possess. This results in the users seeing themselves as 'owners' of the system. In an ideal case, a synergy develops between the users and developers as they jointly attempt to arrive at the most exact description possible of users' requirements and wishes (Dearnley and Mayhew, 1983). The high degree of user involvement also means that they can more easily follow the progress of the development project. The early availability of a prototype and the extensive contact between developers and users during the prototyping process makes the project more visible. All of these factors lead to the user having greater confidence in the information systems department.

Publications about prototyping are, in general, quite theoretical. Practical experience

Table 4.1 Average scores and Mann–Whitney U Test results on users' perceptions of the development process.

	Communication	Participation	Conflicts	Understanding
Prototyping approach	3.86	4.20	1.36	3.66
Conventional approach	3.00	3.21	2.86	2.78
Probability	0.13	0.0014	0.0019	0.11

Source: Adapted from Alavi (1984a), © 1984 Association for Computing Machinery, Inc.

with the approach is still fairly limited and few empirical studies have yet been published. However, it appears that the expectations about the positive influence of prototyping on users' attitudes is confirmed in practice. The few authors who describe practical experiences in this area agree that such positive effects really do occur (see for example: Earl, 1982; EDP Analyzer, 1985).

It is of course impossible to provide hard and fast proof of these effects, since it is a matter of attitudes and perceptions. The cited publications still report subjective views. One of the few studies which attempts to make a more objective comparison, in respect of the users' perceptions of the development process, between the conventional system development approach and prototyping is by Alavi (1984a). He reports a laboratory experiment in which one information system was developed several times, using both conventional and prototyping approaches. The development approach functioned as an independent variable. One set of dependent variables dealt with the users' perceptions of, and attitudes to, the development process. These were measured in terms of:

1. Ease of communication between system developers and users.
2. Satisfaction with the level of user participation in the process.
3. Perception of friction or conflicts between system developers and users.
4. Users' understanding of the development project.

Users were asked to rate their perceptions in respect of these items on five-point Likert-type scales (1 = low; 5 = high). Table 4.1 shows the results. The column headings refer to the dependent variables listed above. The first two lines of this table give the average scores on these four variables. Using a statistical test (the Mann–Whitney U Test), it was checked whether the differences between the pairs of scores in the various columns could be ascribed to chance, or whether the two strategies really differed on the points concerned. The last line of the table gives the probability of the differences measured; when this is less than 0.05 the difference may be termed statistically significant.

It is apparent from Table 4.1 that users belonging to the prototyping groups viewed the development process more favourably on all points in comparison with those users faced with the traditional approach. The statistically significant results indicate a higher satisfaction with the degree of user participation, and a clearly lower level of friction between developers and users. Although the results on the other two

Table 4.2 Average scores and Mann–Whitney U Test results on users' perceptions of the development process

	Satisfaction	Accuracy	User-friendliness	Usefulness
Prototyping approach	4.40	4.06	3.46	4.21
Conventional approach	3.21	2.64	3.07	3.14
Probability	0.011	0.002	0.345	0.007

Source: Adapted from Alavi (1984a), © 1984 Association for Computing Machinery, Inc.

points were not statistically significant, they do suggest that prototyping facilitates communication between developers and users and increases the users' understanding of the development process.

Although the research results may have been influenced by the relatively small sample sizes and the laboratory-like character of the study, they agree fairly well with results obtained in field interviews reported by the same author (Alavi, 1984b). The study thus confirms that prototyping has a positive influence on the attitude of users towards the development process.

SATISFACTION OF USERS WITH THE INFORMATION SYSTEM
On the grounds of the large influence that users exert on the functionality and the user interface of the system under development, it may be expected that prototyping results in more user-friendly products. This aspect was also dealt with in Alavi's study. Among other things, measurements were made of:

1. The overall satisfaction with the finished product.
2. The accuracy of reports produced by the system.
3. The user friendliness of the information system.
4. The usefulness of reports produced by the system.

Table 4.2 shows the average score on the above points and the results of the Mann–Whitney U Test.

The results indicate that prototyping leads to a greater satisfaction with a system than the conventional approach. The accuracy and usefulness of the system's output were both rated significantly higher. This result is confirmed in a study by Längle *et al.* (1984), in which it was established – on the basis of a poll among Fortune 500 enterprises – that prototyping increased the satisfaction with a system for both users and developers.

What is a little surprising in Alavi's study however, is that the systems developed following each of the strategies did not differ very much in respect of user friendliness. This does not agree with the pattern of expectations, since prototyping devotes more attention to the user interface than the traditional approach. The small size of the difference in user friendliness might be a result of the laboratory character of the experiment. All the groups were highly motivated to develop a good product, and it is possible that in the teams that followed the conventional approach there was a more intensive interaction and communication with the users than is usual in this approach.

Prototyping will thus contribute to healing the breach that may have formed between users and systems development staff as a result of previous experience. The use of this requirements definition approach results directly in an improved attitude of users towards the development process. Similar effects can be expected in the longer term. Prototyping results in a significant fall in the maintenance effort required (see Section 2.3). As stated above, the maintenance load is an important cause of long waiting times for new applications. The use of prototyping on a wider scale will ultimately mean that more capacity can be directed towards new development. The information systems department will be able to react more flexibly and quickly to new development requests.

4.3 BOUNDARY CONDITIONS FOR PROTOTYPING

The preceding sections described the criteria for deciding whether it is wise or desirable to use the prototyping approach in a particular problem situation. It is also necessary to investigate whether prototyping is possible. For this purpose, the following factors must receive attention.

4.3.1 CASE tools

The availability of such powerful CASE tools as a relational DBMS, a screen painter, an active/integrated data dictionary and a VHLL (preferably all integrated in one development environment) is essential to successful prototyping. Without such software aids, development of prototypes is too expensive and the speed of reaction to the changing requirements and wishes of the users is unacceptably low. This speed of reaction strongly influences the effectiveness of the prototyping process.

Further, CASE facilities that support structured methods and techniques are required. Without an analyst workbench it is practically impossible to handle structured methods and techniques correctly in a working situation. This certainly applies during the prototyping process, with its emphasis on speed and frequent changes to the system requirements definition. The use of prototyping in no way diminishes the requirement that the final result of the requirements definition phase must be properly documented.

Exactly which CASE tools must be present depends, naturally, on which aspect of the system undergoes prototyping. If the prototype is restricted to the user interface, a screen painter and/or report generator will be sufficient; when it also has to store data, a DBMS accompanied by a data dictionary must be available. Facilities that support methods will always be needed.

Both fourth-generation environments and analyst workbenches contain screen painters, report writers, dialogue managers, and facilities for drawing diagrams and maintaining the consistency of development data. In general, the screen painters, report writers and dialogue managers found in fourth-generation environments are of better quality than those that are part of an analyst workbench. On the other hand, analyst workbenches have more capability for support of structured methods and techniques. This situation is changing rapidly; suppliers of fourth-generation languages are adding facilities to support the earlier phases of a project to their tool sets. The suppliers of analyst workbenches are adding tools for the realization of prototypes, including (simple) DBMSs and fourth-generation languages. Interfaces between analyst workbenches and such tools as COBOL generators are also becoming available.

When selecting the tools to be used during prototyping, an important criterion is the usability of prototypes built with them as the basis for (parts of) the production system. In general, it is wise to choose a technical environment that is suitable for the realization of both prototypes and production systems (such as ADABAS/Natural/ Predict). Alternatively, one could choose a prototyping environment that provides tools for generating, on the basis of the prototype, parts of a production system running in another technical environment.

Part Three goes into extensive detail about fourth-generation languages and analyst workbenches.

4.3.2 Type of system

DATA-ORIENTED VERSUS PROCESS-ORIENTED APPLICATIONS
Prototyping is not feasible without the right tools. This severely restricts the number of systems appropriate to this approach to requirements definition, since the majority of presently obtainable CASE tools are specifically suited to the prototyping of: (1) data-oriented applications which (2) place a major emphasis on the user interface and (3) have a strong on-line character.

When the emphasis is on the processing of the data – the algorithms – rather than on the data itself, the present languages and tools that support the prototyping process usually fall short of what is required. Complex operations cannot usually be properly described in a non-procedural way. The result of a process can sometimes only be described in terms of the process itself; in other words, by indicating exactly what steps must be performed in order to arrive at the result. To be considered for prototyping, the collection of data and the facilities for its maintenance (insertion, modification and deletion) must be the principal components of the system to be developed.

In the current fourth-generation development environment, tools that support the rapid definition and realization of the user interface are found. In some environments it is possible, after the structure of the database has been defined, to generate the screens needed for selecting data from, and for maintaining, the database. This simple user interface can form part of the initial prototype, and, during subsequent iterations, can be quickly modified with the aid of the screen definition facility.

Perhaps the most important reason why prototyping is particularly suitable for systems that strongly emphasize the interface between the user and the system is that, during prototyping, working models serve as a means of communication. The system developer and user discuss the external manifestation of the system and thereby

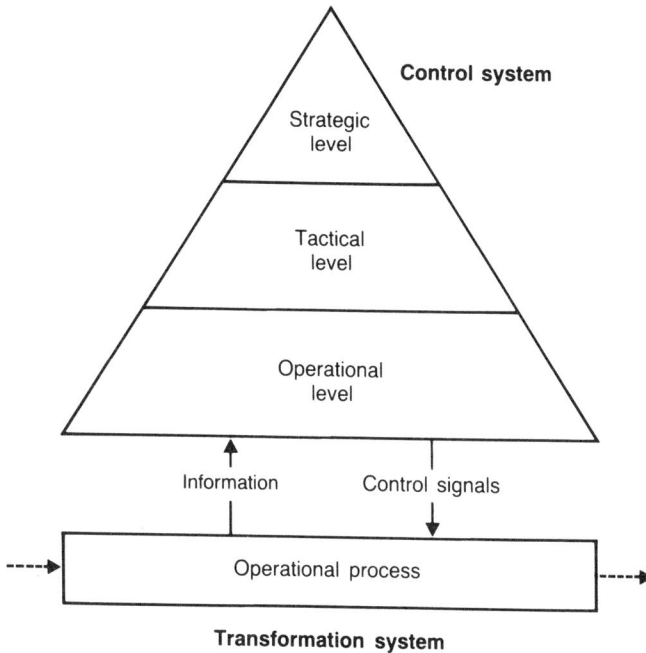

Figure 4.3 Decision levels within an organization.

enlarge understanding not only at the external level but also at the conceptual level. Information systems where the interface between the system and the user is not an important component are ill-suited to an approach to requirement definition that specifically uses this interface as the chief vehicle for discussion.

CLASSIFICATION ACCORDING TO DECISION LEVEL

In the literature it is occasionally stated that the applicability of prototyping is highly dependent on the type of system to be developed. The system typology commonly employed is based on the decision levels that can be recognized in an organization (Fig. 4.3). The following categories are identified.

1. Systems that support or automate the operational process (also known as transformation systems).
2. Systems that support operational management in controlling the operational process.
3. Systems that provide support in planning the operational process at the organization's tactical level.
4. Systems that support strategic management.

At the base of the decision pyramid are those decision-making problems that are relatively easy to formalize and automate. The information needs of the transformation process are stable, routine and limited in scope. At higher levels, the scope of the decisions (and hence the consequences of decisions for the organization) is broader, and the decision maker becomes more dependent on information originating from outside the organization (about economic developments, competitors, etc.). At the strategic level, the need is for heavily compressed and selected data which indicate, at a glance, the state of affairs at lower levels in the organization.

Although the distinction between strategic, tactical and operational management is often not as clear-cut as in this simple model, this typology is useful to divide the information infrastructure of the organization into comprehensible and manageable parts. However, it is doubtful if this classification is useful in determining whether or not to use prototyping in a given situation. At all decision levels in an organization, there may be a lack of clarity about the requirements to be met by the information system. At the base of the decision pyramid, the information problem will tend to be structured; uncertainty about the system requirements at this level will concentrate around the user interface. Higher in the pyramid there is likely to be uncertainty at the conceptual level, particularly concerning the functions that the decision maker wishes to have in the system. At all levels in the organization – though perhaps more often at the tactical and strategic levels – there will be uncertainty about the requirements and wishes, and prototyping can play a useful role.

The limited use of this classification in selecting an approach to requirements definition is also apparent from the fact that various authors take the system type as a decision criterion, but then arrive at contrary recommendations. Thus Boar (1984) advises against using prototyping for decision support systems, and suggests reserving this approach for structured problems; Naumann and Jenkins (1982) state that it is precisely decision support systems which lend themselves to a prototyping approach. Of course, such contrary recommendations could also be the result of the various authors interpreting the terms 'prototyping' and/or 'decision support' in different ways.

BUSINESS VERSUS TECHNICAL INFORMATION SYSTEMS

Another typology sometimes used in selection of a requirements definition approach is the split between *business* (or *administrative*) *information systems* and *technical information systems*. Business processes, and therefore the information systems that support them, are characterized by the management of large quantities of data, and by relatively simple processing requirements. In technical information systems, the real-time aspect is often important, and modelling of processes is more important than that of data structures. In the case of embedded software, there is the further problem that, once this software has been developed on a particular machine, it may need to be ported to different hardware. Another example of software included in the 'technical' category is mathematical software such as linear programming.

The tools needed for prototyping technical information systems are largely unavailable at present; it must therefore be stated that the prototyping approach is currently unsuitable for such systems. In the author's experience, the user interface of technical information systems is often, to some extent, ignored. Where the interface between the user and the machine is an important component of a technical information system, it may be useful to prototype this interface in order to obtain a deeper insight into this area.

4.3.3 Size of system

A widespread misconception exists that prototyping can play no role in the development of large and complex systems. The prime cause of this misunderstanding is probably the stereotype image that is held of prototyping, in which the system developer and the user, sitting together before the screen, quickly develop the complete system. With this interpretation, it is, of course, impossible to subject anything more than the very simplest applications to prototyping.

There is, however, no reason why large-scale applications are unsuited to a prototyping approach as advocated in this book. Its chief characteristic is that it combines the well-known structured methods and techniques with the iterative/heuristic prototyping process. In this way it ensures that analysis of the problem and structuring of its solution receive sufficient attention.

Another factor that makes prototyping worth considering for large applications is that, in a fourth-generation development environment, even large applications can be realized quickly. In practice it appears that with the present tools it is feasible to develop a fully documented initial prototype comprising of between 25 and 35 screens and 40 to 60 on-line programs in a period of four to six weeks (Boar, 1984).

As stated above, when developing an information system it is not necessary to develop the entire system in the same way. A large system usually embraces users and sub-systems of strongly divergent character. In such cases prototyping will be adopted for those parts of the system which (in accordance with the criteria mentioned in this chapter) lend themselves to this approach.

4.3.4 Users and system developers

CAPACITIES AND MOTIVATION OF USERS
Establishing the system requirements definition by use of prototyping is possible only when the models are evaluated by users who:

1. May be considered representative of the entire community of users.
2. Have authority to take decisions in respect of the system requirements definition.
3. Are capable of taking sensible decisions about the requirements definition.

Prototyping places a very heavy emphasis on the central role of the user in the requirements definition process. Perhaps the most important precondition for the success of prototyping is that the user is willing and able to perform the role assigned to him. The user must be capable of arriving at an ergonomically sound user interface that appeals not only to himself, but also to his colleagues. It is the user's responsibility to see that the system is complete from a functional viewpoint, and that it will need no modifications in this respect for some considerable time after it has been installed. Although users know the problem area better than anyone else, not every user is capable of taking wise decisions about the system requirements definition. After all, users are not professional analysts or designers. It takes considerable expertise on the part of the system developers to guide the prototyping process along the right lines.

When the future users of the information system under development hold diverse and conflicting opinions about the functions the system ought to have and its external form, it makes less sense to follow a prototyping approach. Prototyping provides no remedy for structural differences of opinion. However, if the conflict of views is non-structural in character, but is caused by uncertainty about the system's functions and appearance, the development of a prototype can still be considered. This prototype can serve as a basis for discussion among the users, who must try in this way to come to a common standpoint.

There are several conceivable situations in which no representative future user(s) of the system can be found. This will be the case when it is not yet known exactly who the future users will be, or when a very large group of users is involved. This occurs, for example, in the development of an application package.

Prototyping demands much time and attention from the users involved in the process. They have to be prepared for this. They must be willing to spend time evaluating and reviewing the model, and management must make them available to do this. When nobody is available to evaluate the prototype, the prototyping process grinds to a halt.

Application system developers must be aware that users opposed to the introduction of the information system can misuse the prototyping process to cause serious delay to it. Symptoms of this include continually changing requirements and wishes, and users being unavailable at crucial moments. In such cases it can take a very long time for the iterative process to come to a fruitful end. The system developers are then better employed in tracing and analyzing the cause of the resistance, and in removing it. Prototyping demands motivated users who are willing and able to take an active role in the process.

CAPACITIES AND MOTIVATION OF SYSTEM DEVELOPERS

Prototyping makes heavy demands on the capacities of information analysts. They should, of course, possess a good analytical ability, knowledge of structured methods and techniques, the ability to communicate well, and, preferably, expertise in the application area. In addition to the traditional skills of an information analyst, prototyping demands a sound knowledge of what is and is not possible with the available software tools. The prototyper must be able to select the most appropriate software tools from those available, and use them to develop quickly a well-structured prototype. He must also be aware of the problems that can arise during the technical design phase, for example when parts of the prototype which are to form part of the production system have to be integrated with sub-systems developed in parallel along traditional lines or already operational. It is particularly important that the prototyper is aware of any limitations of the target environment, to guarantee that what is modelled in the prototype can actually be realized in the production system.

So, prototyping demands a blend of skills in one person that in the traditional process was spread over several functionaries (information analyst, technical system designer and programmer). However, if no such persons are available, one could think of installing prototyping *teams*, consisting of an information analyst and a technical designer.

Prototyping requires a positive attitude from system developers in relation to users. In the past, it was not unusual for users to be regarded as a tiresome adjunct of the development process. The complexity of the design and realization process meant that attention was not focused on identifying the information problem, but rather on the later phases in the development process. On the premise that the users were incapable of expressing – or even knowing – what they wanted, the system developer made his own assumptions about the nature of the problem and its best solution.

This situation is changing. It is becoming widely accepted that the systems department should provide a service to other parts of the organization; and not the other way round. The central role of the user is recognized, since only the user knows where the actual information problem lies, and must ultimately work with the system. This realization has led to strategies for application system development in which user participation is fundamental; it is certainly a prime motive for prototyping.

To work successfully with these strategies, the system developer has to be 'user oriented'. The developer must take a positive attitude towards the very intensive interaction with the users that characterizes these approaches, and must be prepared to allow the user to control the development process to a significant extent. In prototyping, he must have a positive attitude to the continual changes in the system requirements that are characteristic of this approach, and must even stimulate them. To modify a prototype repeatedly requires a high degree of motivation in the system developers (Podolsky, 1977).

4.4 SUMMARY

The developer of information systems currently has a whole gamut of development strategies, structured methods, techniques and software tools at his disposal. Whenever a new information problem arises, a sensible choice has to be made from this collection. Those who are professionally involved in the development of information systems today may be expected to be familiar with the fundamental differences among the various strategies and methods. The professional system developer must have a well-filled toolkit at his disposal, and must be capable of selecting and using the right tool for a given problem situation.

This book does not aim to give a complete overview of the various strategies, structured methods, techniques and software development aids, and the criteria that must be applied when making a choice among them. Its scope is restricted to the applicability of prototyping in a given environment or problem situation. In the initiation phase of a project, the project leader must decide, on the basis of the criteria described in this chapter, whether a conventional or a prototyping approach is to be adopted for the requirements definition phase. The criteria are summarized below.

COSTS VERSUS BENEFITS
When a prototype can be retained as a basis for the production system, the economic criteria almost always point to a prototyping approach. If the prototype is to be discarded, the prototyping approach should be followed only if there is uncertainty

about the demands the users place on the information system to be developed. This uncertainty depends on:

1. The deducibility of the requirements from the tasks to be supported.
2. The knowledge and experience level of users and analysts.
3. The risk of communication problems.

Prototyping has a number of intangible benefits which should, of course, be taken into account when a choice has to be made between a conventional or a prototyping approach. The most important of these are that prototyping leads to a more positive attitude on the part of users, in respect of both the development process and the information system department, and to a greater degree of satisfaction of users with the information system.

AVAILABILITY OF AUTOMATED TOOLS

CASE tools (workbenches, code generators, VHLLs and so on) raise the efficiency of the development process and make it possible to adapt prototypes rapidly and flexibly to changed requirements and wishes. The biggest pay-off of CASE tools is obtained by using them in a prototyping approach; prototyping without such tools is impracticable. So, prototyping and CASE go hand in hand.

TYPE OF SYSTEM TO BE DEVELOPED

Due to limitations in the fourth-generation development aids currently available, prototyping is at present specifically applicable to: (1) data-oriented applications which (2) place a heavy emphasis on the user interface and (3) have a strongly on-line character.

Where the emphasis lies on the processing to which the data must be subjected instead of on the data and its structure, suitable prototyping tools are not yet widely available. The prototyping approach is currently well suited to administrative information systems and, because of the lack of tools, less well or not at all suited to technical applications.

Selection criteria based on the organizational decision level for which the information system is intended are of little value since uncertainty about requirements may occur at all levels in the organization.

USERS AND SYSTEM DEVELOPERS

The users who take part in the prototyping process must be representative of the community of users and must be able, willing and free to take decisions about the system requirements definition. On the systems development side, the process must be conducted by professional 'prototypers' – people who possess a complex of skills which, during conventional system development, are found in several functionaries and who are strongly 'user oriented'.

Chapter 5

Introduction and Use of Prototyping

The introduction of prototyping into the organization and its subsequent use can give rise to problems. So far, we have sketched a favorable image of prototyping and its effects. The developers, in close cooperation with the users, iteratively build a working model of the system, which results in improved communication between the developers and users, significantly better requirements definitions, a more favorable attitude on the part of users, and so on.

A different situation can also be imagined. In this situation, users not fully acquainted with the aims of prototyping react sceptically to an initial prototype which completely fails to meet their needs; the prototype is so difficult to adapt that there can be no question of rapid iterations; after an arduous and prolonged development process, the users refuse to wait for the production system and will not let go of the prototype (it works, doesn't it?), and so on.

Most of the problems during the introduction and use of prototyping are due to insufficient knowledge of the concepts by both users and development staff, and the failure to follow a phased approach consistently (such as that described in Part Two). This is examined in Section 5.1, summarizing potential problems and describing how they may be avoided. Section 5.2 describes how prototyping can be successfully introduced into the organization.

5.1 POTENTIAL PROBLEMS

5.1.1 Misapprehensions among the development staff

The image of prototyping held by many developers leads to a belief that prototyping is very different from the approaches to which they are accustomed. They may be concerned that all their accumulated knowledge and experience has suddenly become worthless with the arrival of this new approach to requirements definition. Prototyping may be seen as a threat to their status and position. In some cases this will lead experienced developers to reject prototyping. They will appear very sceptical about the approach and may even attempt to sabotage it. In addition, the natural resistance to change must be overcome.

Much of the resistance that occurs among the automation community during the introduction of prototyping is caused by lack of proper understanding of the concept. Education and training can largely forestall this problem. It must be made absolutely clear that prototyping is an evolution of existing approaches to requirements definition, rather than a revolutionary new development approach. Skills developed by working with structured methods and techniques are not discarded with the advent of prototyping; on the contrary, they combine well with this approach and, indeed, are an essential part of it. Prototyping must be seen as an *addition* to the set of strategies, methods and techniques at the disposal of the information analyst, not as a *substitute* for them.

This is not of course, to say that prototyping changes nothing. The application of prototyping requires developers to master new skills and tools (e.g. fourth-generation tools). It also demands a change in attitude to both the development process and the role that users play in it. A developer who aspires to succeed in a prototyping environment must be prepared to change. However, the changes are less extensive than might at first sight be expected (on the basis of many of the publications about prototyping). Therefore, a well-aimed education and training effort can overcome many sources of resistance.

5.1.2 Misapprehensions among management

Managers responsible for controlling project budgets may consider an approach whereby systems (although only simplified working models) are built, revised or replaced a number of times and finally even discarded as a fine waste of time and money. In contrast to these managers, who envisage a cost-inflating effect, there are others who firmly believe that prototyping leads to a considerable increase in the efficiency of the development process, and thus reduces cost.

In Chapter 4 it was shown that each of these opinions represents an over-simplification of the subject. Whether prototyping is justified from a purely economic standpoint will depend mainly on the prospects of being able to use (parts of) the prototype as a basis for the production system, and also on the degree of uncertainty that exists about the requirements for the system. In addition, prototyping has various intangible but very real benefits which must also be taken into account. It is questionable whether prototyping leads to increases in efficiency. Prototyping is primarily aimed at raising the effectiveness of the development project; the increases in efficiency that many people believe they see, in practice are due to the use of fourth-generation languages. The managers in charge must be reliably informed about the costs and benefits of prototyping itself, so that the decision on whether or not to adopt this approach to requirements definition is based on firm grounds.

5.1.3 Misapprehensions among users

False expectations from prototyping may exist among users, largely arising from insufficient knowledge of the aim of prototyping and its effects. This may lead to the choice or rejection of prototyping for the wrong reasons and to disappointment with the approach.

SUITABILITY OF THE PROTOTYPE AS A PRODUCTION SYSTEM

Without proper guidance, inexperienced users tend to expect that the 'definitive' prototype can function as an operational system. It is not clear to them why they have to wait – maybe for a considerable time – before the operational system becomes available. Users are often already very satisfied with the final prototype, and regard it as complete in all respects. This leads to pressure on the developers to close the project and to turn their attention to other systems. This problem appears to occur frequently in practice (EDP Analyzer, 1984).

Premature hand-over of the prototype system to the users may have undesirable consequences. Omission of the upgrading phase means that many factors that are essential to the successful installation and use of a production system will have been neglected. These include:

1. Performance.
2. Exception and error situations and the means of handling them.
3. Back-up and recovery.
4. Security.
5. Reliability.
6. Maintainability.
7. Testing.
8. Documentation, for both users and technical support.
9. Operating costs.

It is highly probable that when a prototype is used as a production system without proper consideration of these aspects, the initial satisfaction of the users will turn, after a short while, into discontent. The failure will usually be ascribed to the development approach used in the project.

It is the responsibility of the prototypers to make the users aware of the limitations of prototypes at the start of the project. It must be clear that after prototyping activity has finished – especially if the prototype is to be discarded – there will still be a lengthy period before the real system will be available for use. A prototype must be seen primarily as the requirements definition of the system, and not as the system itself. The agreements and the grounds for decisions in this respect are recorded in the project plan described in Part Two (Chapter 8).

THE CONDUCT OF THE PROTOTYPING PROCESS

Lack of full understanding of the procedure and the aim of prototyping is another potential source of disappointment. It must be made clear to users that prototyping aims, by the use of working models, to enlarge the developer's understanding of their requirements and wishes. Unless this is made clear, users may adopt an unfavorable attitude towards an initial prototype which corresponds to only a limited degree to the system they are expecting to receive. Users who are about to participate in the process must be made aware that during prototyping the emphasis will lie only on selected aspects and/or sub-systems of the whole system, and that, as part of the process, prototypes may be – and even must be – 'kicked around'.

The speed and ease with which prototypes can be modified may lead the inexperienced user to the false conclusion that production systems can be modified with the same rapidity (Dearnley and Mayhew, 1983). This is a further reason for making the difference between a prototype and an operational system explicit. Production systems, even when they result from upgrading a prototype and are written in a fourth-generation language, are generally many times less flexible than prototypes.

TIME REQUIRED FOR USER PARTICIPATION
The involved users must be fully aware of the central role they will have to play in the prototyping process, and the effort and/or time that participation in the project will require.

Prototyping is only worthwhile when users are motivated to participate actively, when they are allowed to and are capable of taking decisions about the requirements of the system and when they have adequate time to evaluate the prototypes. The users' managers must also realize that effective participation in prototyping means that the employees concerned will have to interrupt their normal activities for considerable periods.

Most of the pitfalls described in this section and Sections 5.1.1 and 5.1.2 can be avoided by adequate education and training of all the parties involved. When considering prototyping it is wise therefore, to make information about this approach to requirements definition available at as early a stage as possible, so that all concerned are well informed of the pros and cons.

5.1.4 Inadequate analysis of the problem

Careless use of prototyping may result in the real information problem not being identified, and in the development of a system that only relieves symptoms. A few important causes of this are discussed below.

INITIAL SOLUTION TOO HASTY
The strong emphasis of prototyping on the rapid creation of an initial solution for the information problem can mislead the prototyper into concentrating on the realization of a prototype before sufficient understanding of the problem has been gained. When the users already know much of what they want this is not necessarily a difficulty, since such a prototype can soon be thrown out and rapid convergence towards a definitive prototype is still possible. However, it is a different matter when the users are very uncertain about the nature of the problem and the form that a solution for it should take, and are still open to (perhaps unintentional) influence from the system developers. In problem-solving activities, people tend to stay close to a proposed solution, a phenomenon sometimes called 'anchoring' (Davis, 1982). Radically different solutions will not be proposed unless the persons concerned already have a clear idea of what they want.

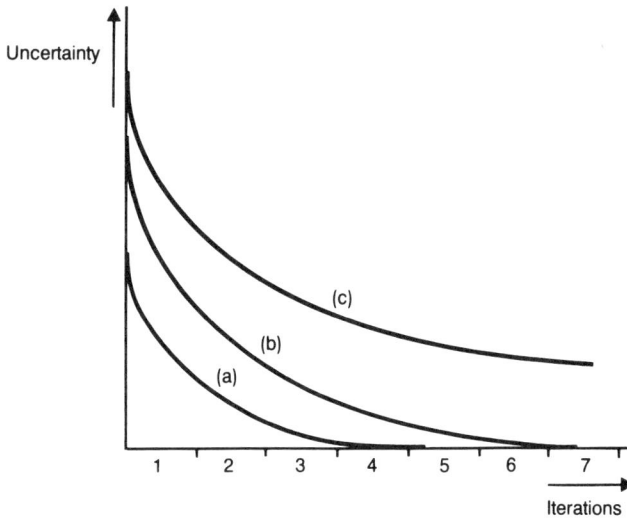

Figure 5.1 Dangers of inadequate problem analysis.

An initial prototype that is not relevant to solving the real problem may have the consequence that either the definitive system turns out to solve the wrong problem, or (in the best case) that the number of iterations taken to arrive at a satisfactory solution is many times higher than necessary. This is illustrated in Fig. 5.1. In situation 'a', a good analysis of the problem was made before building the first prototype. In this case, a rapid reduction in uncertainty about the problem can be seen during the early iterations. The further the prototyping activity progresses, the less the amount of change per iteration. The prototyping activity stops when the prototype is no longer undergoing significant change, on the assumption that users' real requirements have been identified at that point. This assumption is also correct in situation 'b'. However, because of insufficient analysis of the problem, there is still a substantial level of uncertainty present in case 'b' at the start of prototype realization, as a result of which the number of iterations is unnecessarily high. In situation 'c' the prototype ceases to undergo further substantial changes at a point when the real problem has not yet in fact been identified. In such cases, prototyping does not lead to a correct and complete requirements definition.

TOO MUCH ATTENTION TO DETAIL
Prototyping can lead to too much attention to detail in the system under development, with the consequence that there is a loss of perspective over the whole system. Users will be inclined to restrict their criticism to portions of the prototype which they can understand at the time, and – certainly where large systems are concerned – they will have few comments about the place of such parts within the system as a whole. This applies particularly when the prototype is too large in scope to be appraised completely during the evaluation, and when the prototyper has not used a clear structure (e.g. by using hierarchically organized menus).

A problem related to this is the tendency of users to view 'bells and whistles' as being essential to the system, with the result that the iterative process takes too long, the operational system becomes unnecessarily expensive and there is a danger that attention will be drawn away from the primary problem. The cause of this is the speed and ease with which the prototyper adapts the system to new or changed demands and wishes. In order to avoid such situations, the developer must provide a healthy counterbalance. New requirements and wishes should not be accepted indiscriminately; on every occasion, the user and developer must together consider the usefulness of new functions and whether the additional effort demanded to realize them can be justified. It is the prototyper's duty to ensure that a correct balance is struck between attention to detail and attention to the whole.

INSUFFICIENT ATTENTION TO INTERFACES

When insufficient attention is paid during the first rough analysis to the interfaces between the system under development and other systems, problems will be inevitable during the integration phase. In a comparative study by Boehm *et al.* (1984), systems developed using prototyping appeared more difficult to integrate than systems developed according to the traditional approach. The principal cause of this lay in the absence of interface specifications.

Problems of this kind can largely be prevented during the analysis phase by studying the information flows between the system to be developed and the consumers or suppliers of information, with the aid of a good information analysis method (e.g. Chen's (1983) entity-relationship diagramming). In the case of a large or complex system, the traditional top-down activity or process analysis methods (e.g. Structured Analysis and Structured Design) are used to identify reasonably autonomous sub-systems of manageable size. Then, again, the information flows among the various sub-systems must be analyzed.

The goal of prototyping is to improve insight into the requirements and wishes of users in respect of (facets of) the system. If the input is intended for, and/or the output comes from, an existing information system, it is already known exactly what information must be produced and/or accepted. Prototyping cannot play a role here; only thorough analysis of the interfaces can prevent integration problems. Prototyping is applicable only to interfaces between information systems and users and not to interfaces with other systems.

CONFUSION OF PROBLEM ANALYSIS WITH PROBLEM SOLUTION

The traditional approach to the development of information systems places firm emphasis on the stringent separation of problem-oriented and solution-oriented activities. The problem-oriented activities ultimately result in models that indicate what the information system must do and contain in order to solve the discovered problems; concentration is focused on the problems and needs of the users. Solution-oriented activities establish how a system (automated or otherwise) can be realized which satisfies the various requirements and wishes of the users. During design of the solution, the possibilities and limitations of the various software tools become relevant. Some of the arguments for the rigid separation of problem analysis and problem solution are:

1. Requirements definitions must in no way be influenced by constraints resulting from the present technical environment (hardware, operating software, development tools and the like). A requirements definition represents precisely the requirements that the information system must satisfy to solve the problem. When only some of the functional requirements are translated into the design of the system, it is a logical consequence that the problem will not be solved completely. Following this line of thought, the hardware configuration should be a direct derivative of the defined requirements, and is irrelevant during the requirements definition phase.
2. A requirements definition that is independent of the technical environment in which the system must be realized remains valid, even when changes occur in that environment. The requirements definition forms a stable point of departure for the design and realization of the system on, theoretically, any hardware; it is, so to speak, portable.
3. Strict separation of analysis of the problem from design of a solution ensures that both aspects are given sufficient attention, and is a guarantee against thinking in terms of solutions before the problem has been defined. The information analyst can concentrate solely on the requirements problem. The resulting requirements definition then forms a stable point of departure for the designer. Within the framework formed by the requirements definition, the designer has the freedom to consider various solutions and to choose the best.
4. The future users of the system are generally not interested in technical considerations and details. It is, in fact, of no interest to them how the system is constructed. They will wish to view the design and realization process as a *black box*, with a requirements definition as input and an operational system meeting these requirements as output.

Prototyping, at first sight, makes it more difficult to maintain a strict separation between problem analysis and problem solution. After all, prototyping introduces working models – solutions to the problem – during the requirements definition phase. This gives rise to the fear in many people that prototyping will nullify all the advantages of strict separation of definition and design.

A closer examination of the approach shows that this is not necessarily the case. During prototyping, problem and solution-oriented activities are fairly strictly separated (see the five-step approach presented in Part Two). It is, of course, true that the limitations and idiosyncrasies of the tools used to realize the prototype influence the requirements definition. However, this is not a problem since users have the last word about the acceptability of the prototype (and thereby the requirements definition). After all, if the users completely, and with full understanding, accept the system requirements definition, it matters little how this was achieved.

It should be remarked that, although strict separation of definition and design is a worthy ideal, in practice overemphasis of this ideal is unrealistic. An organization is usually committed to a particular hardware and system software strategy; any change to this strategy is unwelcome and very expensive. There is a price-tag attached to every functional requirement or preference. A realistic approach to the requirements definition phase must at an early stage take into account both technical feasibility and cost. A comparison of costs and benefits shows whether the requirement is economically justified, and should be included in the system requirements definition. Thus, some degree of intermingling of the analysis and design processes may even be advantageous. Prototyping gives developers a more realistic view of the effort needed to realize functions, and enables them to verify at an early stage that they can be realized.

5.2 THE INTRODUCTION OF PROTOTYPING INTO THE ORGANIZATION

Acceptance of prototyping as a real alternative to the traditional way of defining requirements is very dependent on the way in which prototyping is introduced into the organization. One way of ensuring that prototyping will fail is to start using it in any project that happens to look suitable, without making thorough preparations. The adverse experiences undergone in such circumstances will guarantee long-lasting hostility to the approach. The introduction of prototyping into the organization must be carefully prepared and planned, and properly supervised.

Before wide-scale implementation can begin, sceptics must be convinced of the usefulness and value of prototyping. Theoretical dissertations are not enough; the value of prototyping will only be accepted after the successful conclusion of a practical test. For this reason, pilot projects are indispensable. Before starting one, the right initial conditions must be created. These considerations lead to an approach phased as follows:

1. Preparation of the organization.
2. Selection and execution of pilot projects.
3. Wide-scale introduction.

These phases are discussed in the following sections.

5.2.1 Preparation of the organization

A smooth and successful introduction of prototyping largely depends on three factors:

1. The attitude of management towards this approach to requirements definition.
2. The training and information effort accompanying the introduction.
3. The availability of suitable tools.

Before practical testing of the approach in a pilot project begins, attention must be paid to each of these critical success factors.

SUPPORT FROM MANAGEMENT
An absolute precondition for the success of any innovation in the organization is a positive attitude on the part of management, who must be strongly motivated to

change the status quo. If support, commitment and dedication from management are not given, any attempt to introduce prototyping is doomed.

Given the problems facing the typical information systems department, its management will generally be willing to innovate. A high level of maintenance effort and the accompanying application backlog sufficiently illustrate that the present way of working is inadequate. It will be clear to management that something must change. However, the best way of tackling the problem, and the measures which will have most effect, will often be much less clear. In Chapter 2 we argued, in this connection, for a combined attack on four fronts: end-user computing, application packages, CASE tools and prototyping.

The support and commitment of the responsible managers can be obtained only when they are fully acquainted with the prototyping concept. As described in Section 5.1.2, it is probable that there will be misunderstandings about this approach. A good formal presentation of the concept and its background can succeed in transforming the initial scepticism into enthusiasm. This presentation can also function as an occasion for obtaining formal approval for a practical evaluation of prototyping and for the expenditure this will entail. At the very least, the points that must be dealt with are:

1. The principal causes of the application backlog, the weak and strong points of structured methods and techniques and the way in which prototyping complements these (Chapter 2).
2. A broad description of the prototyping approach (Chapter 3).
3. The cost/benefit effects of prototyping (Section 4.1).
4. The preconditions for prototyping (Section 4.2).
5. The proposed evaluation method, and its costs (Section 5.2).

EDUCATION OF ALL PERSONNEL INVOLVED

At least as important as obtaining management support is informing and training users and development staff involved in the pilot project. In Section 5.1, detailed attention was given to the consequences of insufficient knowledge of the prototyping concept: resistance on the part of development staff and exaggerated expectations on the part of users. Therefore, everyone must be aware of the goal of prototyping and the consequences that implementation of this approach will have for the individual's role in the development process. The organizational climate, seen in terms of developers' and users' attitudes, must be favorable to prototyping. Users must be motivated to make the effort that prototyping will demand. Developers must take a positive attitude towards this approach, which will after all have significant consequences for the way in which they work. Education and training will play an important role in the cultivation of a climate well disposed to prototyping.

Information analysts who are going to work as prototypers must acquire practical skills in the use of CASE tools. They must be able to create a working model quickly using the DBMS and data dictionary system (DDS), the non-procedural language used in the environment concerned and the screen-definition and report-generation facilities. They must also be comfortable with the analyst workbench (if available).

Because of the differences between prototyping and the traditional approach to information system development, established standards, norms and procedures may prove restrictive in the prototyping environment. For example, one potential source of conflict is the role of the database administrator in the development process. Traditionally, the database administrator approves the database design before any actions are taken actually to create the database concerned. Prototyping demands an early realization followed by continual, rapid modification of the initial database, and in this there is no place for time-consuming, formal procedures. In prototyping, the database administrator is required only to approve a database design which will be implemented in a production system; he is involved in the development process in a different way, thus making it necessary to revise the existing procedures.

Potential points of friction must be anticipated, and those responsible for the supervision of standards and procedures must be made aware of the consequences of the prototyping approach. Although it is fairly obvious that the introduction of prototyping entails the modification of standards, it appears that people are not sufficiently aware of this in practice (Alavi, 1984b).

PROTOTYPING TOOLS

Prototyping will fail if the necessary CASE tools (including a preferably relational DBMS, a non-procedural language and a good screen painter/report generator) are not available. It is pointless to attempt to introduce prototyping into an organization which does not yet work with such tools. The presence of a DDS – integrated with the DBMS – will simplify the development of prototypes, as will a good analyst workbench.

The introduction of such tools into the organization will generally be independent of the introduction of prototyping. These tools are aimed at raising the efficiency of the development process and they can be used within several development approaches – including the conventional linear one. As we have said, more efficient development is one of the potential avenues of escape from the 'software crisis'. The greatest benefit resulting from the use of CASE tools is, however, obtained in combination with prototyping.

It is important for the prototyper not to be hindered by hardware restrictions. There should be an (intelligent) workstation for each prototyper and ample internal and external storage. Response times must be good. Office accommodation is also important; to allow communication with end-users to proceed undisturbed, the developers must have the use of a suitable meeting space, preferably containing presentation facilities such as large-screen projector.

5.2.2 Selection and execution of pilot projects

After a good starting point has been established for a practical evaluation, the next step is to select a suitable pilot project (or a number of projects). Circumspection must be exercised in making this choice; when the system selected does not lend itself to prototyping, the result will not only be failure or disappointment, but probably also the unjustified rejection of prototyping. In selecting pilot projects, the following criteria should be used:

1. *Type of system.* This has already been discussed in detail in Section 4.2.2. As a consequence of the characteristics of current CASE tools, prototyping is particularly applicable to the development of information systems in which much attention must be given to the user interface. When the emphasis lies on the processing that the data must undergo, there are at present no well-suited means available for the rapid realization of prototypes.
2. *Size of system.* In general, both large and small applications may be prototyped (see Section 4.2.3). However, the size of the system to be developed is a factor in selecting a pilot project. The application must be large enough to demonstrate that the approach is applicable to development of large systems, but not so large that the prototypers, who are still gaining experience, encounter problems on account of the size of the project. The visibility of the project in the organization (there will be many interested spectators) is a further reason for choosing one that is not too large, so that the first results will appear quickly.

Before starting the pilot project, it is important to define the criteria that will be used to evaluate it. After successful conclusion of the pilot project, it will have been demonstrated that a good requirements definition or, if the prototype can be upgraded, an operational system can be produced by prototyping. Through the pilot project, sceptics can be convinced that the approach is feasible and practicable, and that it produces results. However, because of the absence of objective criteria for evaluation, it is impossible to measure the quality of these results. On the basis of maintenance costs, it should be possible to obtain some insight into the effectiveness of the system. In a pilot situation, however, it will rarely be possible, for practical reasons, to use the system for an extensive period in order to measure maintenance costs. So, it will be difficult to demonstrate objectively whether financial benefits have accrued in comparison to the traditional approach. Furthermore, the results of a traditional approach (whether or not in combination with a fourth-generation language) in the project concerned are unknown.

The criteria that can be used in evaluating the pilot-project results will, therefore, be largely subjective. Examples are: the degree of satisfaction of users with both the process and the resulting product, the appreciation of developers for this approach to requirements definition, and the impression that project management has of the course taken by the project and its final results. It is desirable that the people involved already have experience of the traditional approach, so that they can make proper comparisons.

It must be realized that a project which deviates from well-trodden paths runs a higher risk of failure than a conventional one. If the pilot project produces disappointing results on specific points, this is not necessarily because of the development approach used. The causes may also lie in insufficient experience with the new way of working, or lack of proficiency in the use of the tools. The risk of failure can be reduced by giving the prototypers the chance to run through the whole process with a small test problem without any interaction with users before starting the pilot project. In the pilot project it is important to be able to concentrate on the evaluation of prototyping, without being distracted by other innovations in the development process. When an attempt is made to introduce new structured methods, new tools and a new development approach simultaneously, and additionally to venture into an unknown application area, failure is almost inevitable.

5.2.3 Dissemination of the prototyping approach

When the pilot project concludes with a recommendation that prototyping should be accepted as a fully-fledged alternative to the traditional way of establishing requirements, and management agrees with this recommendation, it must be considered how to broaden the basis of prototyping within the organization.

Before selling the prototyping approach, the right conditions for its successful application must be created. A practical manual, tuned to the needs of the organization, must be produced. The standard project model must be modified to allow prototyping in the requirements definition phase, and to permit the prototype to be used as a basis for the production system. Training courses must be developed for both project managers and developers. Organizations or departments about to work with prototyping for the first time must be able to call upon consultants with experience of this approach.

In a small organization, everyone will be aware of the pilot project and its results. If the people involved in the pilot project are enthusiastic, others will need little urging to use prototyping. In a large organization, the pilot project will often be carried out by a corporate department with responsibility for selection and standardization of development methods, techniques and tools.

Before prototyping can be applied on a wide scale, a considerable public relations effort – dependent on the size of the organization and the authority of the methods department – will have to be made. Prototyping must be properly sold, so that the broad support essential for its real acceptance is obtained.

Chapter 6
Concluding Remarks

There can be no doubt that prototyping is an important development in the field of information system development. It leads to further professionalization of the development process, through the introduction of something that in other engineering disciplines is already common currency: working models of the system to be developed. With prototyping, automation acquires a 'friendlier face' in the eyes of the users, so that this requirements definition strategy contributes to narrowing the gulf between users and information systems specialists.

In Part One we have pointed out several times that there is little empirical material available on the effects of prototyping. Although the author's practical experience supports the thesis that the effects mentioned in this book really do occur, there is still a lack of 'hard' proof. The present chapter will discuss a number of matters that ought to be researched further.

EMPIRICAL RESEARCH ON PROTOTYPING

The analysis of the *cost/benefit effects* of prototyping in this book has, as already stated in Chapter 4, a fairly tentative and qualitative character. An empirical foundation is needed for the following:

1. The effect of prototyping on *development costs*. It may be expected that prototyping leads to an increase in development costs, and to delayed project completions. This hypothesis is primarily based on the fact that prototyping must be regarded as a supplement to, and not as a replacement of traditional methods and techniques. Even when a prototype can be retained as the basis for the production system, a project using prototyping for requirements definition will probably cost more than conventional development, since the process is an iterative one. It would be useful if this supposition were supported by hard figures.

   Making measurements in this area is difficult. The most significant stumbling block is that the costs of software development depend on a very wide variety of factors. To make reliable assertions about the effect of prototyping on the development process, either research will have to take place under very closely controlled 'laboratory' conditions, or a very large number of observations will have to be made.

2. The effect of prototyping on *maintenance* costs. It is still unclear whether the

expectation that prototyping leads to requirements definitions of better quality than the traditional approach is justified. Again, there is an absence of hard figures. Unfortunately, a good yardstick for the quality of requirements definitions is not readily available. However, it is possible to obtain some insight, since there is an inverse relationship between the magnitude of the maintenance costs and the quality of the system requirements definition. The effects of prototyping should be noticeable mainly in the maintenance phase.

However, in measuring the effects of prototyping on maintenance costs one is again faced with the problem that there is a very large number of cost drivers. To isolate the effects of prototyping, it will again be necessary to perform a large number of observations. Research of this kind is expensive and must extend over a very long period. In fact, measurements must be continued until the systems 'expire'. To establish exactly what influence prototyping has on maintenance costs therefore demands exceptional perseverance. Laboratory research can hardly be considered as an alternative to observation, since the object of interest is the use of a system in practice over a considerable length of time. It is well-nigh impossible to keep all the interfering factors stable for a sufficiently long period.

3. The effect of prototyping on *user attitude* towards both the development process and the developed product. In Chapter 4 we referred to a study by Alavi on this subject. This is one of the very few studies where an attempt has been made to obtain some empirical foundation for the expected effects of prototyping. In this research, it appeared that prototyping did not lead to systems that were significantly more user-friendly. Such surprising conclusions call for further study.

It is a challenge to both the academic world and to the practicing community to come to a better empirical foundation for the points described above. In particular, empirical research into the cost/benefit effects of prototyping is expensive and time consuming. Cooperation and exchanging of information between the various research agencies and the business community are essential for deepening insight into this matter.

RELATED RESEARCH ACTIVITIES
In this book, many subjects that have points of contact with prototyping have been mentioned briefly in passing. Several of these topics do not receive enough attention in the current literature. Some research activities which should take place in the short term are:

1. Development and application of a *contingency approach* for choosing development strategies, methods, techniques and automated tools, for both project control and development activities. In this book attention has been paid particularly to the criteria that may be used in choosing between prototyping and a traditional approach. This must be seen within a broader context: a project leader has other choices to make too. In practice, there is an urgent need for a comprehensive framework that facilitates the choice between:

    (a) end-user computing or development by information system specialists;
    (b) purchasing a standard package or in-house development of the system;
    (c) the development approach to be followed (participative, evolutionary, prototyping, linear, process-oriented or data-oriented, and so on);
    (d) the structured methods, techniques and CASE tools to be used within a given approach.

2. Evaluation of the *productivity effects* of strategies, methods, techniques and software tools. Currently, there is a totally inadequate understanding of the business reasons for introducing new development tools into an organization. Prototyping is not the only requirements definition strategy about which there is insufficient quantitative data available. In the field, people often indiscriminately follow the fashionable trend of the moment, without a careful prior analysis of whether this is justified from the point of view of costs/benefits. The literature offers few leads; statements on productivity are generally qualitative, and when quantitative statements are made they are all too often inadequately supported by evidence. Research into the productivity effects of the various development strategies, methods, techniques and tools (fourth-generation or otherwise) is urgently required.

3. Taking stock of the *problems of introduction* of new development strategies, methods, techniques and tools. In practice it appears that the introduction of (for instance) structured methods or fourth-generation tools is frequently far from simple. In the field of management science, much attention has been paid during the last few decades to the management of processes of organizational change. The possibilities for applying this knowledge to the introduction of systems development strategies, etc. have – as far as the author knows – not yet been systematically investigated. The literature and the suppliers of new CASE tools should devote more attention to this subject.

FINAL REMARKS

The discipline of information system engineering is still young and is developing vigorously. As yet, there is no sign of a firmly established terminology. There are hardly any 'established truths' in this field; practically everything is open for discussion. The rapid developments in hardware are an incentive for developments in methodology, which in their turn lead to identification of needs in the province of technology. Prototyping is a good example of a 'technology-driven' development; the direct stimulus for the inception of this strategy for requirements definition lies in the arrival and growing popularity of fourth-generation tools.

In this dynamically developing discipline, it is useful and necessary to take an occasional step back. In this chapter, a number of points for reflection have therefore been mentioned. It is wise to take a critical attitude towards new developments; too hasty an introduction of all kinds of novelties can lead to problems, since it can overload the organization's capacity to absorb them. On the other hand, too much delay in the introduction can ultimately harm the competitive position of the enterprise. Part One of this book has attempted to make a reasonable case for the proposition that the time is ripe to introduce prototyping.

Part Two

A Detailed View of
the Prototyping Process

Chapter 7
Introduction to Part Two

Many authors have sung the praises of prototyping. The literature on this subject gives an impression that prototyping has made the development of information systems many times simpler and cheaper. The suggestion that the conventional approach and its associated structured methods and techniques can be thrown away remains unspoken, but often lies just below the surface. Since very few authors have published anything more than a very broad description of the prototyping process, the exact source of the claimed advantages is not clear.

A closer look at the subject reveals that this is a case of the proverbial thought, and its equally proverbial father – the wish. It is naive to suggest that anything other than the most elementary applications can be developed without any prior analysis by the user and the developer sitting together at the terminal; and it requires boundless optimism to suppose that a system developed in this way could function successfully in practice.

Part Two explains how the principles of prototyping can be combined with conventional methods for analysis and design of information systems to produce a balanced whole. The proposed mixture of rigour and trial-and-error approaches enables the developer to profit both from the strong points of the conventional methods and from the advantages of prototyping. Prototyping does not imply a revolution in the way information systems are developed, in the sense that all the old methods may be thrown out; it would be more reasonable to speak of an evolution, building on the basis of conventional practices.

Part Two is arranged as follows: Chapter 8 briefly describes the main issues dealt with in the *pre-project* and *initiation phases*, which include finding out whether prototyping is the best requirements definition approach for the problem. Using prototyping has particular consequences, especially for the execution of the *requirements definition phase*, so the description of this phase in Chapter 9 provides the bulk of Part Two. In Chapter 9, a separate section is devoted to each of the five sub-phases of the prototyping approach to requirements definition. At the end of the requirements definition phase, there is not only a system requirements definition available, but also a working prototype. Chapter 10 investigates the consequences of this approach for the *further course of the project*. For each phase and sub-phase dealt with in Chapters 8 to 10, we describe the goals, the activities and the criteria for moving on to the next stage. Chapter 11 is a concluding summary. Figure 7.1 depicts the structure of Part Two. As the reader may find this figure useful as a guideline, it is repeated at the beginning of each chapter and section.

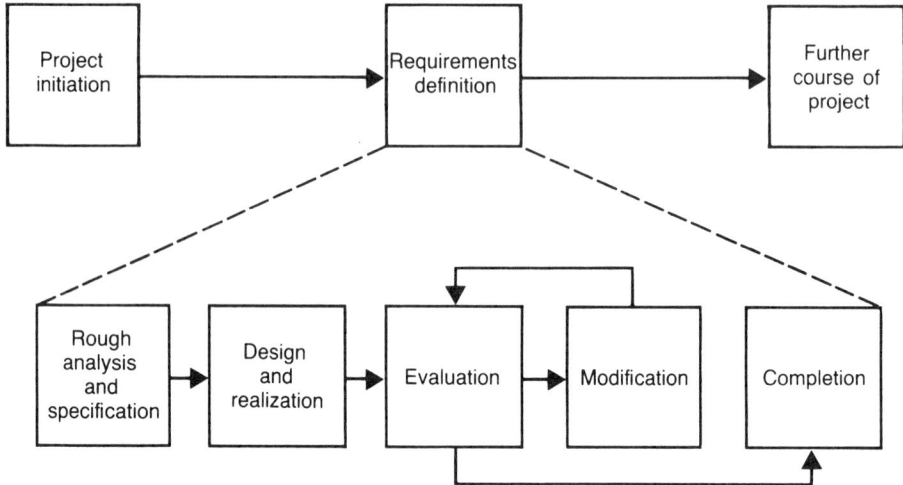

Figure 7.1 Structure of Part Two.

In Chapter 3 we explained that prototyping is aimed at clarifying the users' requirements in respect of specific *aspects* and/or *parts* of the planned system. It is possible to develop some sub-systems using prototyping, and others in a conventional way. Equally, there will be situations where the uncertainty relates only to a specific aspect (for example, the user interface), so only that aspect is modelled during prototyping. Part Two describes how to proceed when *functional* prototypes are developed. On the basis of this description the reader will be able to work out how the simpler forms of prototyping can be integrated into the development process. We shall not deal with the situation where some parts of a system are prototyped while other parts are handled separately in a conventional way. This situation does not add any extra complications when proper attention is paid to the specification of the interfaces among the various sub-systems early on in a project.

The reader should be aware that the phased structure presented in Part Two is only one possible way of dividing the development activities into phases and sub-phases. Furthermore, this model is, like the familiar 'waterfall' model of the software development process (and indeed any model), an abstraction and idealization of reality. Generally, there will be a large number of feedback loops between the (sub-) phases. Project models such as this serve two main purposes: to give project management a means of *controlling* the process, and to make the process *surveyable* and thus *teachable*.

Chapter 8

Project Initiation Phase

8.1 GOALS

The project initiation phase is the first step that must be taken after a user department has submitted a request for application development. The chief goals of this phase (see Fig. 8.1) are:

1. To arrive at a (rough) demarcation and description of the business problem, and a broad indication of its solution (the development of an information system, or other measures).
2. If the development of an information system is decided on, to structure the project and to choose the development strategies, methods, techniques and software tools to be used.

Increasing numbers of organizations have specified information systems architectures

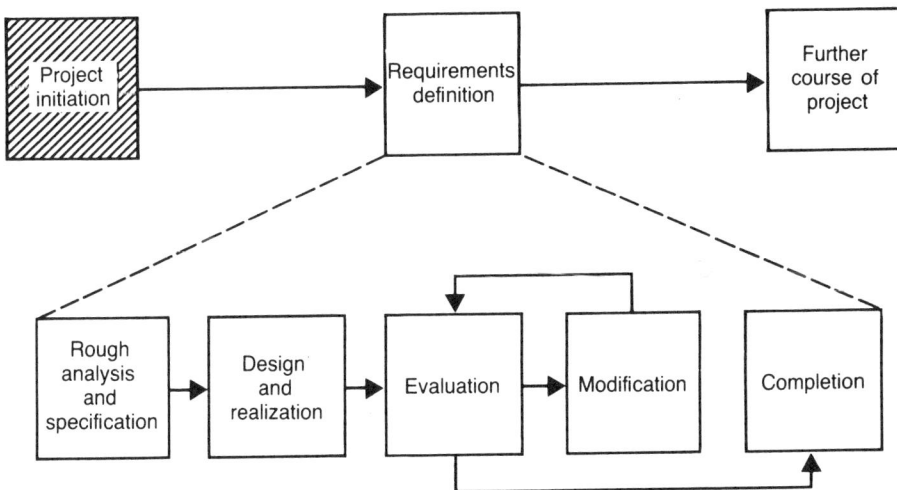

Figure 8.1 Place of the project initiation phase within the development process.

and, on that basis, have planned which development projects are to take place, in what order, for a number of years ahead (Martin, 1982b). The work to be done in step '1' of the project initiation phase depends on the amount of detail in these plans. Step '2' will generally not have been dealt with in an information plan.

8.2 ACTIVITIES

This sub-section describes the activities to be performed during the two distinct steps of the project initiation phase (demarcation of the problem and selection of a development strategy).

DEMARCATION OF THE PROBLEM

Interviewing the intended users is the information analyst's primary means for obtaining insight into the problem area during the project initiation phase. The interviews result in an outline of the existing situation and an inventory of the problems. It is important at this stage to try to penetrate to the core of the problem. All too often it becomes apparent only after the end of a project that the solution arrived at relieves the symptoms, but does nothing to cure the disease.

After the information analyst has described the problems and their causes as accurately as possible, the changes needed to resolve these problems are investigated. Assuming the problems really do concern the information infrastructure, we can broadly classify these changes into two categories:

1. Improving the information infrastructure by developing an information system (automated or non-automated), or by modifying an existing information system.
2. Changing the organization; the way in which an organization is structured has a very considerable influence on the information which its individual component groups need in order to function satisfactorily (see for example: Galbraith, 1973).

The process of describing and analyzing the problem situation and outlining the desirable changes is sometimes called 'change analysis'. The procedure to be followed during this change analysis has been admirably worked out within the ISAC method, which is widely used in Scandinavia and the Netherlands (Lundeberg *et al.*, 1981). Naturally, techniques for activity modeling other than the ISAC 'activity diagrams' can be used as well during change analysis. Examples of similar techniques are the SADT 'activity graphs', the 'dataflow diagrams' used in the Yourdon methodology, and the variants of the ISAC 'activity diagrams' such as those to be found in IBM's SASO. The various modeling techniques of this kind differ little from one another in expressive power and representational possibilities.

It would be going beyond the scope of this book to indicate how to proceed when the appropriate solution to the problems is to change the organization itself. For a description of the various alternative organizational structures, the reader can consult Galbraith (1973 or 1977), for example. The characteristic problems associated with organizational change and possible strategies for dealing with these problems have also been described extremely well elsewhere (see for example: Schein, 1969). Below, we describe the procedure to be followed when it becomes apparent from analysis of the problem situation that development of an information system is the appropriate answer, and a project is initiated as a consequence.

SELECTION OF A DEVELOPMENT APPROACH

Chapter 4 summarized the criteria for choosing between prototyping and conventional approaches for requirements definition. When a prototyping approach is selected, it is important to decide at the same time whether, in principle, the prototype should go on to function as a basis for the production system or it is to be discarded. This makes the situation clear to everyone involved, and pre-empts some potential problems (see Section 5.1). This decision has important consequences for the cost/benefit analysis and for the time between the conclusion of the prototyping phase and the availability of the production system.

Whether a prototype can function as a basis for the production system depends primarily on the quality of the CASE tools used in the prototyping process. If experience shows that satisfactory production systems (meeting stringent demands for performance and quality) can be efficiently developed with these tools, it will not be necessary to re-build the entire information system in a more efficient language after prototyping is complete.

8.3 CONCLUSION

The project initiation phase finally delivers a *project plan*. This document may be regarded as an initial contract between the users and the developers, and as such forms a stable basis for the further progress of the project. The project plan makes it clear to all parties involved what the problem is, how this problem is to be tackled and what tasks and responsibilities are assigned to everyone concerned in the development process. Through this, the development process is made transparent; those involved know what they may expect from one another, and when. The project plan comprises at least:

1. A concise description of the present situation, of the problems present in that situation, of various alternative solutions and the solution chosen.
2. A definition (preferably short and trenchant) of the aim of the project.
3. A description of the development strategy or strategies, methods, techniques and software tools to be used by the system developers, and the grounds on which these choices have been made.
4. A summary of the products with which the various phases are to be concluded.
5. A description of the project organization: the composition of the steering committee and the project team, and the role and responsibilities of both system developers and users during the development process.
6. A time schedule and an estimate of costs and benefits.

When a prototyping approach has been selected, it must be clearly stated within the project organization that the users who form part of the project team must be available to evaluate the prototype. The users are responsible for the timely and clear formulation of criticism, requirements or wishes that become apparent in the course of using the prototype. The choice of prototyping as the approach for requirements determination will also have direct consequences on the deliverables and the expected distribution of effort and costs during the project.

The project initiation phase is concluded when the project steering committee formally approves the project plan.

Chapter 9

The Requirements Definition Phase with Prototyping

The aim of the requirements definition phase (Fig. 9.1) is to arrive at a complete, consistent and accurate record of all the requirements and wishes that users have with regard to the information system under development. This phase is problem-oriented; attention is focused on deeper analysis of the problems described broadly in the project plan, and on detailed definition of requirements and wishes with respect to the solution. How the solution can (or must) be realized is a matter for the design and realization phases, which can be described as solution oriented.

This division into problem-oriented and solution-oriented phases is, to some extent, an idealization of the real situation. Even during the requirements definition phase it is, of course, important to take the technical possibilities into account. This implies that a rough technical design must be drawn up before the definition phase can be concluded. It is becoming widely accepted that, in reality, the system requirements definition is influenced by technical limitations. Thus, although the emphasis during the definition phase remains on the problem, an eye must be kept open for potential and practical solutions. Prototyping fits exactly into this outlook. The specific goal

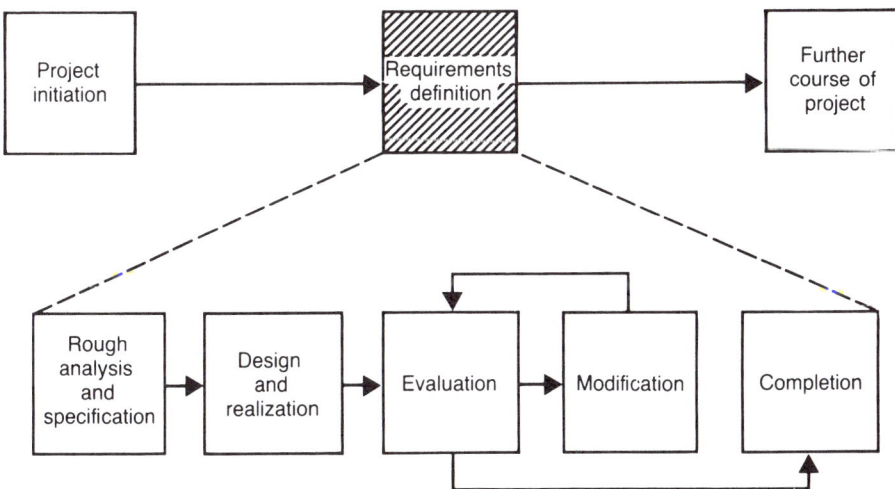

Figure 9.1 Place of the requirements definition phase within the development process.

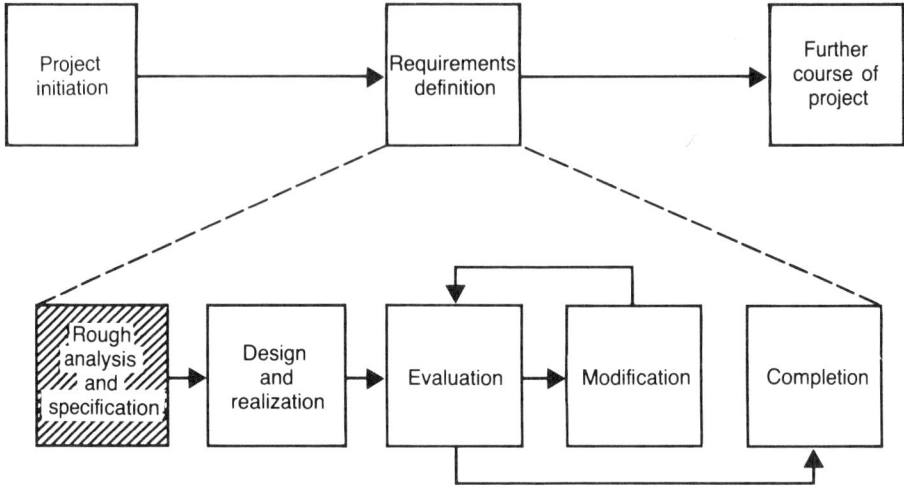

Figure 9.2 Place of the rough analysis and specification sub-phase within the development process.

of prototyping is to establish a system requirements definition, but, because working models have to be built, it leads at the same time to an improvement of insight into the technical possibilities and limitations.

This chapter describes the course of the requirements definition phase when a prototyping approach is adopted. Obviously, the project initiation phase may conclude that a conventional approach will be the best way to achieve a complete and correct system requirements definition in the given situation. The conventional approach has already been exhaustively explored by many authors (see for example: Cutts, 1987; DeMarco, 1978; Gane and Sarson, 1979; Hatley and Pirbhai, 1987; Page-Jones, 1980; Ward and Mellor, 1985; Yourdon and Constantine, 1979) and is therefore not considered further in this chapter.

9.1 ROUGH ANALYSIS AND SPECIFICATION

9.1.1 Goals

The rough analysis and specification sub-phase (Fig. 9.2) aims to arrive at a stable basis for prototype design, realization and iteration. Before design and realization can be started, there must be sufficient understanding of the problem. It is important that the first prototype does not fall too far wide of the mark, with undesirable consequences for both the efficiency and the effectiveness of the development process (see Section 5.1.4). When prototyping is adopted, attention must still be paid to analyzing the problem and defining the requirements and wishes for its solution. The iterations during prototyping aim to refine and complete the requirements definition rather than build it from scratch.

9.1.2 Activities

This sub-phase strongly resembles the conventional requirements definition phase. The information analyst uses the same modeling techniques, relying either on abstract models for communication with users, or on natural language if the users do not understand these models. However, there are some important differences from the conventional requirements definition phase:

1. The rough analysis and specification sub-phase results in provisional specifications. In all probability, these will be adjusted several times during the prototyping process. It is accepted that the provisional specifications, as a consequence of the imperfect communication means available to the information analyst at this stage, will almost certainly contain errors and omissions. The verification of these specifications takes place through the use of prototypes.
2. The amount of detail aimed at in this sub-phase depends on the uncertainty in the situation concerned. This is related to the complexity of the problem, the level of knowledge and experience of users and analysts, the likelihood of communication problems between users and analysts, etc. (see Section 4.2.1). During the sub-phase it must be continually considered whether, on balance, it makes more sense to continue the analysis or to develop a prototype in order to obtain a deeper insight into the problem and its desired solution.
3. Attention is here focused on the functionality that the system must supply to the user. Performance requirements (response times, reliability, back-up and recovery, etc.) are not considered in this sub-phase. By the time the requirements definition phase in total has been concluded, the inventory of such requirements must, of course, be complete.
4. In contrast to the conventional requirements definition phase, here there is no intention to arrive at a complete external specification of the information system (dialogue structure, screen layouts, etc.). At the conclusion of the prototyping process, the system developers and users should be in complete agreement with regard to the user interface, but insight into external aspects of the system is mainly gained through the use of prototypes, that is, only after the conclusion of the rough analysis and specification sub-phase.

A possible set-up of the rough analysis and specification sub-phase is described below. Many variants of this are conceivable. This section gives a general indication of the way in which structured requirements definition methods can be applied within the prototyping approach. Naturally, an organization's usual way (including its methods and techniques) for dealing with the requirements definition phase and the technical design and realization phases can be retained within the prototyping process.

1. (ROUGH) ACTIVITY ANALYSIS

The first activity in this sub-phase is to define the boundaries of the system by modeling that part of the organization which the new information system is intended to serve (in ISO terms: its environment). Both existing and desired situations should be modeled. It is worth modeling the existing situation to ensure a common understanding of the problem area.

This activity results in a model of the activities of the relevant part of the organization, and of the exchange of information among them. Sufficient insight must be obtained to establish which activities can be formalized and thus automated. The information analyst takes a top-down approach to this, making it possible to achieve a sufficient level of detail without losing sight of the whole. Examples of diagramming techniques supporting this approach are dataflow diagramming and SADT's activity diagramming.

2. (ROUGH) INFORMATION ANALYSIS

Information analysis aims to give the system developer insight into that part of the world – the 'universe of discourse' – about which the information system is intended to supply information. This activity results in a model of entity types and the relationships among them (the 'entity-relationship' or 'information structure' model), and the most important rules applicable to those entity types. Entity types, associations and rules are established by analyzing the information flows among the activities identified in the previous step. This leads to a clearer insight into the activities of the organization, which may in turn stimulate modification or extension of the entity-relationship model. There is a strong interaction between information analysis and activity analysis.

Examples of methods for information analysis are Chen's entity-relationship modelling (Chen, 1983) and Nijssen's NIAM (Wintraecken, 1985), both of which operate at the conceptual level – as is appropriate during the analysis phase. Aspects of form are of no account early in this phase; they may impede the information analyst in analyzing the problem. The analyst will consider how the user wishes to see the information presented (the format of the data, etc.) only after a clear understanding at the conceptual level has been achieved. In this sub-phase, the analyst establishes what the system is about and what it should do, but not how it should look.

Although errors and omissions in the entity-relationship model can be corrected during iteration, the analyst should aim here to form a picture of the real world that is as error free and complete as possible. On the basis of the information analysis, a database will be designed and implemented during the next sub-phase (design and realization). It is important that this database – the 'heart' of the system – achieves maximum stability as soon as possible. It is then possible to experiment freely with the way and the form in which the end-user can manipulate the stored data, without having to repeatedly restructure the database. Prototypes serve as a means of verifying the correctness and completeness of the information model, and of the database structure based on that model.

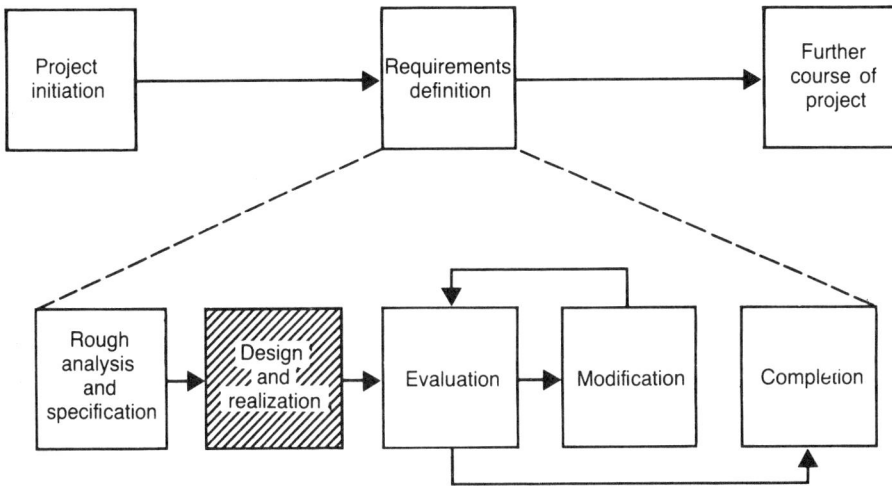

Figure 9.3 Place of the design and realization sub-phase within the development process.

9.1.3 Conclusion

The rough analysis and specification sub-phase results in a provisional requirements definition for the information system. The diagrams produced will generally provide adequate documentation for this sub-phase. The provisional requirements definition comprises at least:

1. A description of the activities and information flows in the part of the organization that the information system must support (for example in the form of dataflow diagrams several layers deep).
2. An outline of the automated functions that the information system must provide.
3. A outline of the important entity types and associations among them (the entity-relationship model), and the most important rules applying to the universe of discourse.

If required, the provisional requirements definition can be submitted for approval to the users. However, formal approval at this stage is not essential, as there will be ample opportunities to adjust the specifications during prototyping.

9.2 DESIGN AND REALIZATION

9.2.1. Goals

The objective of the design and realization sub-phase (Fig. 9.3) is to obtain, within a reasonable time-span, an initial prototype. During this sub-phase, the prototyper concentrates on supplying a system with maximum functionality, rather than on creating an optimal user interface from an ergonomic point of view. Optimizing the way the system presents itself to its users is a task of later evaluation and modification sub-phases; first, consensus must be achieved on functional aspects. Issues such as performance and reliability should generally not be considered here.

During the design and realization sub-phase, there need be little or no discussion with the users involved in the project; development takes place on the basis of the understanding of the problem that was built up in the preceding sub-phase. A prototype soon becomes too complex or too comprehensive to be developed by the prototyper and the user sitting together in front of the screen, as the stereotype image of prototyping would have it. Naturally, the developer could immediately consult the user on any points which may be unclear or inconsistent.

9.2.2 Activities

In the design and realization sub-phase, attention is focused successively on the design and realization of the database, on the dialogue structure and on the functions to be performed by the system.

1. DESIGN AND REALIZATION OF THE DATABASE

In order to arrive at an optimal structure for the collection of data, normalization principles are applied (see for example: Codd, 1970; Kent, 1983). By normalizing the data model, it is possible to forestall inadvertent redundant data storage. Consequently, fewer problems arise when the contents of the databases are updated. In a fully normalized structure, each item of data occurs only once so that when changing that item of data there is no chance of creating conflicts (by failing to change the same item of data in other places). If it later becomes attractive for performance reasons to store certain items of data more than once (to 'de-normalize' the database), measures can be taken to keep the database consistent during updates.

Based on the normalized data model, the database structure is designed. If a relational DBMS[1] is used, this takes little effort; every entity type (or, in relational terms, 'relation') in the data model is simply translated directly into a table. This will not be the optimal database structure from a performance point of view, but performance is not important at this stage. The emphasis must lie on maintaining maximum flexibility. After all, it is possible – although not particularly desirable – that the database structure will have to be modified several times during the prototyping process. For this reason, a simple direct translation of the normalized data model into a relational database structure is chosen.

When a network DBMS is used, the design of the database structure is only a little more complex. Again, the most direct possible representation of the normalized data model is chosen in designing the network schema. In this schema, every entity type in the data model is mapped on to a record type. However, connections between record types must now (unlike in the relational model) be explicitly indicated by the inclusion of owner–member relations, or sets. To complete the network schema the designer must define the sequence in which the records are stored in the logical chains, the way of selecting the chain in which a record must be stored and the nature of the relationship between owner and member.

Before realization of the designed structure can be started, the designer has to add information to the relational or network schema about the type and length of the various attributes or fields. The actual realization then requires the database schema to be described in the data description language (DDL) of the DBMS, and compiled.

2. DESIGN AND REALIZATION OF THE DIALOGUE STRUCTURE

In the rough analysis and specification sub-phase, a provisional list was made of the functions to be performed by the system. Here, these functions are incorporated in menus. Menus are a suitable interaction mechanism particularly for inexperienced users of the system (Shneiderman, 1980). There is no need for the user to think of the command or function key needed to invoke a required action, and it is clear what actions are possible at any given moment. This makes menus extremely useful as the interaction mechanism in prototyping, during which the system is still liable to continuous change. As the user accumulates experience with a system, repeated passage through the menu tree often becomes a source of irritation, and the user will prefer more direct access to the available functions, for example by means of a command language. Exploration of the user's requirements concerning the interaction mechanism is relevant only later in the prototyping phase; at this stage, menus are usually adequate.

While the prototyper is designing the initial dialogue structure, there are some ergonomic/design considerations that have to be taken as a starting point. These are as follows:

1. A menu should always give the user the option of returning to a previous menu, and the user must be able to jump back directly to the top of the menu tree. It may be worth allowing jumps freely from any menu to any other. Every menu should include the options 'help' and 'quit' (Fig. 9.4).
2. If the number of options on a menu becomes too large, the designer should consider removing some options and creating a sub-menu for them, invoked as an option on the original menu. As a guide the *maximum* number of options per menu should be the same as the number of function keys.
3. A standard layout is recommended for all menu screens. In this way, the various applications with which the user is confronted are given a degree of uniformity and familiarity.

Menus can be produced quickly with the aid of a screen painter. The links between the individual menus can be implemented using the facilities of the fourth-generation environment or workbench. This, again, is fairly simple; displaying a new menu involves only retrieving and displaying a previously created screen. Some fourth-generation environments and workbenches include special facilities for modeling and realizing menu structures.

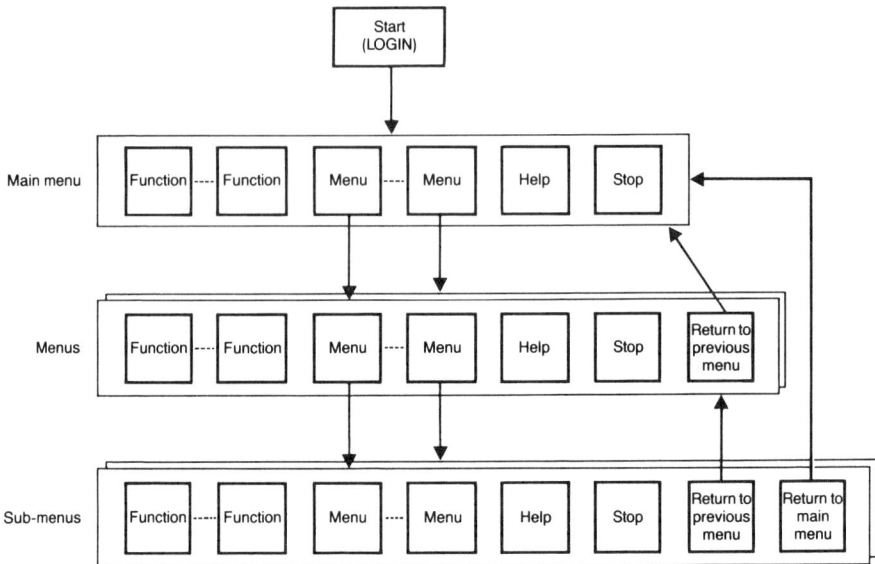

Figure 9.4 The general structure of a menu tree.

3. DESIGN AND REALIZATION OF FUNCTIONS

Each function offered in the menus consists of two parts: the part that handles the interaction with the user, presents the results of a selection operation on the database, etc. (the user interface), and the part that actually operates on the data. In user-interface prototyping, only the former part of the functions (about which there is uncertainty) is designed and realized. In functional prototyping, some real functionality is also added to the prototype.

Functions can be broadly divided into two categories:

1. Functions for maintaining the database (adding, modifying and deleting data).
2. Functions for reporting on the contents of the database.

The functions in the first category are developed using the screen painter and fourth-generation language facilities available in the CASE environment. The screens are based, as far as possible, on the structure of the database. A screen is created for each table (record type), containing all the attributes in that table. All functions aimed at maintaining the table can then, initially, use the same screen.

It is advisable to standardize the layout of the screens. This has the advantage that the user rapidly becomes familiar with the application (knowing always, for example, where error messages will appear on the screen). Furthermore, this reduces the screen design effort. There are guidelines and draft standards for screen construction available (see for instance: Smith, 1986). By following such guidelines, ergonomically sound user interfaces can be constructed quickly and easily.

The database structure has been recorded in the data dictionary during step one of the design and realization sub-phase. In an integrated development environment, the screen painter consults the data dictionary during screen creation, and the developer does not have to respecify attributes. In some fourth-generation environments it is possible to generate default screens for input, modification and display of data from the database, based on the database structure described in the data dictionary. The screen painter can then be used to implement refinements (such as displaying attributes in reverse video or in a frame). It often enables the implementation of validation checks on input data; this is usually limited to specifying permitted values. Some advanced screen painters can handle more complex rules. In an ideal case, any rules specified through it should be stored in the data dictionary, so that they can be automatically enforced whenever the data concerned are modified via other screens or by programs. However, few of the existing fourth-generation products have this sophistication; it is generally left to the developer to ensure that complex validation rules are obeyed.

The second category of functions provides reports on the database contents. In fourth-generation environments, and in some advanced workbenches, reporting and analysis facilities are available. Many of the desired reports can be created quickly with the aid of a non-procedural language coupled to a report generator. The developer specifies the data to be selected, and the report generator determines a suitable report layout. At this point in the prototyping phase, the developer will make little use of the facility for modifying the default layout. Presentation requirements will be dealt with later; here the developer checks only that he is on the right track in terms of functionality.

9.2.3 Conclusion

The design and realization sub-phase is concluded when a prototype, providing sufficient material for discussion with the users, is ready. This may occur as soon as the menu structure has been implemented; more usually, it will be when a proportion of the functions offered on the individual menus has been realized.

This sub-phase results in a *working prototype*, together with a *provisional design* of the system consisting of:

1. A database design, based on the normalized provisional data model.
2. An outline of the menu structure.
3. An outline of the implemented functions, including a description of the structure of the more complex functions.

It is not necessary to document this separately. The database design is well documented in the data dictionary. The prototype itself serves as documentation of the menu structure and of the implemented functions.

9.3 EVALUATION

9.3.1 Goals

The primary aim of the evaluation sub-phase (Fig. 9.5) is to establish that the system requirements definition (as embodied in the prototype) is stable and detailed enough to support further development of the information system. In this sub-phase, it becomes apparent whether the system developers have correctly interpreted the requirements and wishes expressed by the users. Errors can still be corrected easily and cheaply. Users become acquainted with the prototype and adjust the system requirements definition as a result of the experience they have obtained and of their deepened insight into their own requirements and wishes. A prototype thus serves two ends: it is a means of *eliciting* system requirements and of *verifying* that developers and users have understood each other properly.

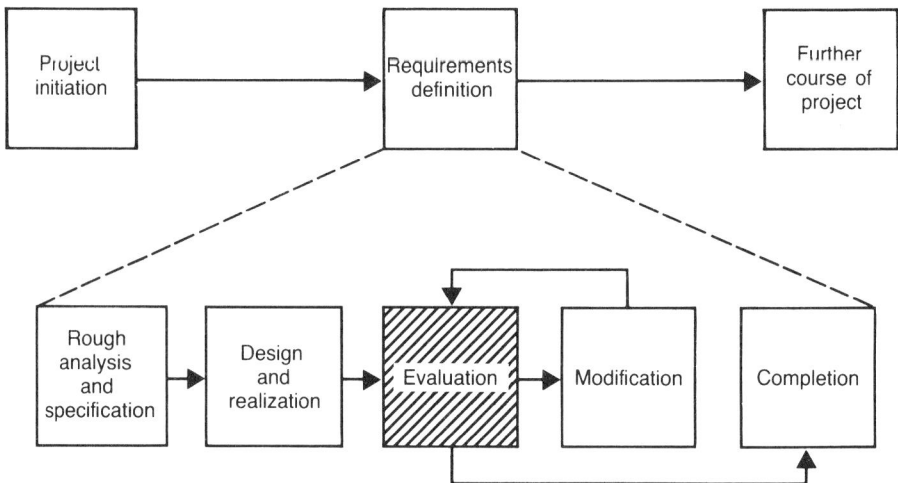

Figure 9.5 The place of the evaluation sub-phase in the development process.

The evaluation sub-phase may conclude that the prototype must be modified. In that case, the iterative process so characteristic of prototyping begins. The prototype is repeatedly modified and re-evaluated until the system requirements definition is stable. In practice, there are usually no more than five iterations. To achieve this, the users involved must be aware that the aim is to produce a good requirements definition as quickly as possible. Iterations cost money and mean that the installation of the completed system will be delayed. Users must strive to minimize the number of iterations; they must not regard prototyping as a licence to change their minds continually.

9.3.2 Activities

Four steps can be distinguished in the evaluation sub-phase: preparation, demonstration of the prototype, use of the prototype and discussion of comments. It is not always necessary to draw hard and fast lines between each step. In general, the boundaries will become less distinct as the number of iterations increases – as the system requirements definition stabilizes. Eventually, the evaluation and the modification sub-phases (discussed in Section 9.4) become merged. Changes to the prototype are then so small that they can be made immediately. Aspects of the prototype may also have been demonstrated during the preceding sub-phase. We emphasize again that the phased structure is an idealized model of reality.

1. PREPARATION
Before demonstration and use of the prototype, all those involved must be aware of the procedure to be followed, the contribution each is expected to make, and the schedule. A date for conclusion of the evaluation sub-phase should be agreed before this point, so that the users involved in the project are clearly aware at an early stage how much time evaluation will require. It is worth distributing parts of the documentation relevant to and readable by the users (an outline of the prototype in the form of a menu structure, examples of reports, etc.) before the presentation. In this way, the users have the opportunity to prepare. This documentation should be accompanied by a checklist summarizing the points that merit special attention during the evaluation.

The contents of this checklist depend on the number of iterations that have already taken place. In the first evaluation pass, attention will usually be focused on conceptual aspects. Here the prototype is used to check, for example, whether any entity type or attribute type has been overlooked during the analysis sub-phase. As already stated, it is of great importance that the database structure stabilizes as early as possible. Of course, the checklist should not contain jargon terms such as 'entity' and 'attribute' unless the users are familiar with them. Rather, such questions as 'Is everything you want to know about an order present on this screen?' should be asked. Next, the developers and users should check if any functions have been overlooked. In later iterations, users will pay particular attention to the user interface. Then the relevant issues are the interaction mechanism, the dialogue structure and the layout of the screens. Figure 9.6 gives a broad indication of the points that merit special attention during successive passes of the evaluation sub-phase.

2. DEMONSTRATION OF THE PROTOTYPE
Demonstration of the prototype takes place on the basis of a scenario drawn up in advance by the prototypers. This scenario includes a broad description of the functions that will be dealt with, and in what order. The making of this plan obliges the prototyper to prepare the demonstration thoroughly. The scenario ensures that everything that must be dealt with during the demonstration will be demonstrated in a well-considered and logical order. Without it, there is a real risk that the course of the presentation will be dictated by questions from the users. Interruptions can, for example, lead the presenter into demonstrating the functions for generating reports

Evaluation phase

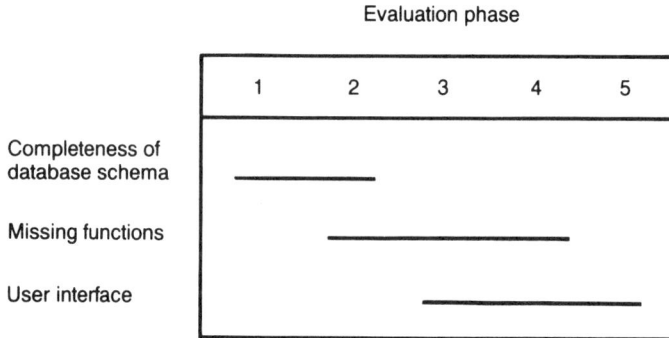

Figure 9.6 Points for attention during successive iterations.

on the database contents before any data has been entered, ('Yes, that's possible too – let me show you . . .'). A well-planned scenario, presented without deviation, ensures that the product will be properly understood by the audience. It is a good idea to hold a rehearsal of the scenario prior to the actual demonstration; as well as being a good preparation for the demonstrator, it provides an opportunity to eliminate any flaws. At the start of the demonstration, the scenario is handed out to all present, making clear what is to be expected and thereby pre-empting many questions about the contents of the demonstration. The hand-out also serves as a useful *aide memoire*.

As a rule of thumb, a demonstration should not run for more than an hour. If a demonstration cannot be completed within this time-span because of the size of the prototype, it is advisable to have this evaluated in parts. A prototype that cannot be dealt with in one hour is too extensive and/or too complex for good evaluation. The users obtain insufficient perspective and do not get to know the prototype well enough to formulate properly founded opinions about all its parts.

During the demonstration, comments will be made about the prototype. At this stage, discussions should be limited to clarification of any misunderstandings about it in its present form. Comments and criticisms are noted and perhaps briefly discussed; the full discussion will take place in step four of the evaluation sub-phase, after users have had the opportunity to gauge properly the value of the prototype.

A valuable aid during the demonstration, especially with a large audience, is a large-screen projector, which enables a workstation image to be projected on to a large screen. A thoroughly professional presentation is a valuable aid to gaining user confidence.

3. USING THE PROTOTYPE
After the prototype has been handed over, the users are given enough time to use it, to become familiar with it, and to formulate well-considered opinions about its usability. If possible, the prototype is immediately tested in a working environment (*shadow running*). It is important that the users involved have enough time reserved for evaluation. The dedication with which they fulfil their task at this stage strongly influences the success of the prototyping process.

While the prototype is in use, attention should be particularly directed at the points included in the checklist, which is drawn up by the prototypers before each iteration. This checklist describes points about which, in the prototypers' opinion, there is most uncertainty at that time. As described in step one, in the early iterations these will be mainly conceptual aspects; later, attention will be focused on such aspects as presentation and external design.

The duration of this step will depend on the extent to which the system requirements definition has already taken shape. In general, as the number of iterations increases the requirements definition stabilizes and users will need less time to evaluate the prototype. When the prototype is no longer subject to major changes, this step may even become unnecessary. The users can ventilate their comments and criticisms during the demonstration, and these can be reviewed immediately.

4. DISCUSSION OF COMMENTS

As a final step in the evaluation sub-phase, observed problems and suggestions for improvements are reviewed in a meeting of users and prototypers. By reference to the checklist, it can be seen whether there are user comments relating to all the points about which the prototypers were unsure at the start of the iteration. The problems, suggestions and questions are discussed in detail, resulting in an outline of changes to be implemented by the prototypers. On the basis of this outline, it must be decided (see Section 9.3.3) whether it is necessary to modify and re-evaluate the prototype. If so, the prototypers estimate when the new prototype will be ready, and a demonstration date is agreed with those involved.

9.3.3 Conclusion

The evaluation sub-phase is concluded when users and prototypers agree about the list of changes that must be made to the prototype. At this point, there are two possibilities:

1. The list of changes to be made is of such a size that it makes sense to modify the prototype, and then have it re-evaluated. In this case, the *modification sub-phase* follows (see Section 9.4).
2. The list of changes to be made is restricted in size, and relates mainly to points of detail (such as the position of a field on a screen). There is hardly any uncertainty remaining about either the functionality that the system must offer or the form it must take. In this case, the *completion sub-phase* follows (see Section 9.5). In the completion sub-phase, attention will be focused on topics related to characteristics which have, thus far, been put aside (e.g. performance, security).

In the first of the above cases, there are two possible approaches to documentation. If good workbenches are available, consideration may be given to adapting directly the documentation produced in the rough analysis and specification sub-phase. With modern software tools, changes can be made with little effort. It is not necessary to keep the documentation continually up-to-date during the iterations. The latest version of the system requirements definition can be reconstructed at any time from the original definition and the changes made during the iterations, and particularly from the prototype itself. When a workbench is not used, repeated updating of documentation will demand (too) much time. In this situation, it is advisable to defer documenting the system requirements definition until it has stabilized.

In the second case, enough clarity has been obtained about the aspects or parts of the information system under consideration. The definitive system requirements definition should now be prepared. For this purpose, first there should be a review and updating of the documentation that was produced during the rough analysis and specification sub-phase (or the last evaluation sub-phase if updates were made during the prototyping process). Then a complete description of the user interface (dialogue structure, screen and report layouts) is added; a large part of this description can be obtained by making prints of the individual screens. Using the prototype itself as documentation of the user interface may also be considered. The choice between these alternatives depends largely on the organization's standards for system documentation.

The prototype itself must be well documented, particularly when it is intended to be the basis for the production system. If an advanced CASE environment has been used during prototype development, most of the required design information is already present in the data dictionary. If the required documentation is not yet available, the present database structure and the program structure of the individual functions must be documented. Sometimes, local documentation standards make it necessary to produce a 'provisional design' document; in other cases, the design information stored in the data dictionary suffices. The design is qualified as 'provisional' because performance, quality and other requirements to be considered in the completion sub-phase will probably make it necessary to change it in several respects.

9.4 MODIFICATION

9.4.1 Goals

In the preceding sub-phase, the requirements definition of the system was modified. Now the prototype has to be changed both so that it can once again be verified that system developers and users have fully understood one another and so that the users have obtained a sufficiently clear insight into their own requirements and wishes in respect of the information system. In the modification sub-phase (see Fig. 9.7), the aim is to implement the changes agreed during the evaluation process within the time-span agreed for this purpose.

9.4.2 Activities

In the early cycles through the modification sub-phase, the prototype may be changed substantially. To maintain a reasonable structure in these circumstances, it will be

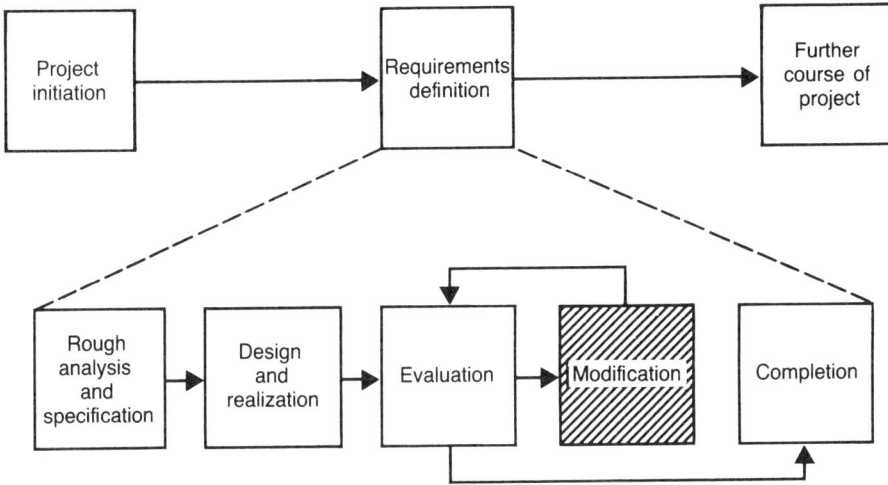

Figure 9.7 The place of the modification sub-phase in the development process.

necessary to redesign parts of the prototype. It is of course particularly unwise to start coding immediately, certainly when radical changes are involved; the advice 'think first, then act' applies as much during prototyping as at any other time.

Depending on the contents of the change list drawn up during the evaluation sub-phase, attention is directed to change and/or extension of the database structure, to the functionality offered by the prototype or to the user interface. As described in the previous section, as the project progresses the centre of interest will gradually shift from conceptual matters (the functionality that the system must provide) to the form that the system must take. The modification sub-phase shows considerable similarities to the design and realization sub-phase (Section 9.2), but not all aspects of design and realization may require attention.

The speed with which modification of the prototype takes place will depend on the quality of the CASE tools used. For example, it is crucial whether or not there is available an integrated data dictionary in which the relations between all the system components are recorded. Such a dictionary makes it possible for the prototyper to determine very quickly what consequences a change to one part of the model will have on other parts. Thus, for instance, when changing the length of a field it is possible to check which screens and reports will have to be modified in consequence.

The flexibility of the DBMS with which the prototype was built is also an important factor. When a relational DBMS is used, extension or modification of the database structure is generally easier than when a network DBMS is used. When schema changes are required in a network DBMS, it is often necessary to stop the whole system, compile the new schema, and dump and restore the entire database, or parts of it (Date, 1982).

9.4.3 Conclusion

The modification sub-phase is concluded when all the changes agreed between users and prototypers have been made. Its result is not only a revised prototype, but also a design that has been changed in various respects. After this, a new evaluation sub-phase begins (see Section 9.3).

Where a good, integrated fourth-generation development environment is used, the contents of the data dictionary will be updated more or less automatically. If good CASE tools are not available, it is inadvisable to undertake extensive documentation of the design at this stage, since the evaluation sub-phase may result in further changes to the prototype – and hence to its documentation. The latter is better deferred until the system requirements definition is reasonably stable and the prototype is not likely to undergo many changes.

9.5 COMPLETION

9.5.1 Goals

The preceding sub-phases have resulted in a complete and stable definition of the functionality that the system must offer its users, and of the way in which it will present itself to them. However, little attention has so far been paid to another important part of the requirements definition – performance and quality. The definition of requirements in this area is not, after all, the primary aim of prototyping. Prototypes are well suited to modelling the form and function of the system; they are not the best medium for modelling requirements for reliability, performance, security, etc. The completion sub-phase (Fig. 9.8) aims to define the requirements and wishes in these respects.

9.5.2 Activities

The contents of a system requirements definition, as defined in the local standards, should now be compared with the system requirements definition available at the end of prototyping. This comparison will show what activities must still take place to complete the requirements definition phase. In general, the following points are likely to need further attention:

1. *Reliability*. A risk analysis must be carried out to check the consequences of stored information being lost, or of a temporary malfunction of the system. On the basis of risk analysis, the reliability requirements of the system can be determined and the consequent test plans for the system can be made. Related to this, the requirements for back-up and recovery (back-up frequency, retention period of data and so on) must be determined. It is also necessary to specify

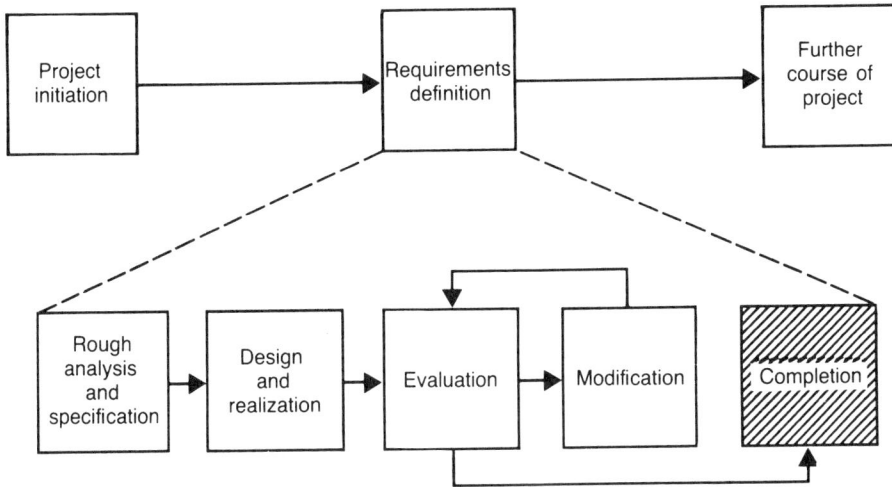

Figure 9.8 The place of the completion sub-phase within the development process.

what measures must be taken to ensure the accuracy of data (completeness and integrity checks, probability checks, etc.), how error handling will be carried out and what reaction is required in exceptional situations.

2. *Performance.* The acceptable response times must be established. Related to this, a survey must be made of the number of users who will make simultaneous use of the system, the normal and peak load on the hardware, the quantities of data to be input and output, the frequency with which that occurs and the anticipated growth.

3. *Security.* It is necessary to define the requirements placed on the system from the point of view of safeguarding the company's interests and information. It must be determined who has access to specific kinds of information, and what kind of authorization (none, read-only, modification) the individual users have. A decision must be made as to whether it is necessary to register who has obtained access to the database, when that took place and what changes were made (an audit trail). The authorization procedures to be followed by the users must be established.

4. *Hardware and software constraints.* The technical boundary conditions under which the system will operate must be defined. If not already decided, it must be established on what machine the production system will run, under which operating system and text-processing monitor, whether there are any requirements in respect of the DBMS to be used, and whether there are constraints in respect of available memory.

It is very important to pay proper attention to these requirements. The developers may be inclined to overlook these aspects, especially when the prototype is to be used as the basis for the production system. Their inclination will be to move directly to the implementation of the system in the organization – a way of working which guarantees the ultimate failure of the project. A prototype is not a production system. Only a system that satisfies the requirements regarding quality and performance identified in this sub-phase will be able to function successfully in an operational situation.

9.5.3 Conclusion

To conclude the system requirements definition phase, the requirements definition drawn up in the final evaluation sub-phase is completed by the addition of requirements and wishes related to performance and quality. A plan is made for the further development of the system with an estimate of the costs still to be incurred. The steering committee is then asked to approve these documents formally.

The system requirements definition documents the agreement between users and developers; it is the basis for the contract between the developers and users for further development of the information system.

NOTE

1. Readers who are not familiar with DBMS of the 'relational' and/or 'network' type are referred to the standard work by Date *An Introduction to Database Systems* (1982).

Chapter 10

The Further Course of the Project

10.1 GOALS

The remainder of the system development process aims to realize an information system that complies with all the defined requirements. In the conventional development approach, the next activity is design, followed by realization of the system. When a prototyping approach is adopted for the requirements definition phase, together with a system requirements definition, a prototype that may already satisfy a large part of those requirements is also available. Thus, there is an alternative to the traditional design and realization phases; the prototype can function as the basis for the production system. As noted in Chapter 4, this way of working will lead to considerable savings in the design and programming phases.

Both in the literature and in practice, there are proponents and (often intense) opponents of the use of the prototype as the basis of an operational system. The opponents consider that a prototype should always be discarded after the prototyping activity, or, at best, that it may be useful as documentation of the production system. They base this standpoint on the observation that a prototype often fails to meet the performance and quality requirements of a production system. The proponents, in contrast, seem unaware of these restrictions. To them, the prototype already offers a great deal of the functionality required by the end-users of the system and they overlook, in their enthusiasm, that performance and quality requirements exist.

Each of these views is partly right. It is true that a prototype generally fails to satisfy the demands made on an operational system, but it cannot be denied that a considerable portion of the system may in fact already have been realized in the prototype. It is, therefore, always advisable to consider carefully whether the prototype, which may represent a considerable investment, can be used in the realization of the production system. The cost of a complete redesign and reconstruction of the information system should be compared with the cost of upgrading the prototype. Often large parts of the prototype can be retained as components of the production system, especially when high-quality CASE tools used during prototyping can also be used for the development of production systems. In such a situation, it would be an unjustifiable waste to throw away the prototype without further consideration. Equally, considering the restrictions of prototypes, it would be irresponsible to treat the prototype as it stands as an operational system.

The remainder of this chapter describes the 'upgrading' phase, in which a prototype

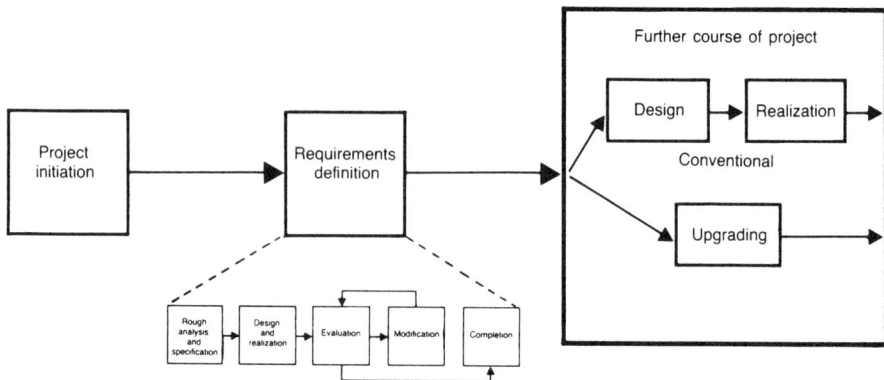

Figure 10.1 Alternatives after conclusion of the requirements definition phase using prototyping.

considered to be suitable as the basis of the production system is made to function as such. This is the most logical sequel to a requirements definition phase in which prototyping is adopted. Where there are valid arguments for dispensing with the prototype in spite of the above considerations, and for designing and constructing the system afresh on the basis of the system requirements definition, the project follows the traditional path through design and realization. Figure 10.1 shows the courses of action that may be followed after conclusion of the prototyping activity.

The basic decision on whether to retain the prototype as the basis for the production system is taken during the project initiation phase (see Chapter 8). However, this decision must not be allowed to influence the prototyping process unduly. The primary aim of prototyping is, and remains, the reduction of uncertainty about the system requirements definition.

10.2 ACTIVITIES

Production systems, whether based on prototypes or not, have to satisfy *all* the requirements established in the requirements definition phase. In the upgrading phase, particular attention will generally have to be paid to:

1. *Performance*. As stated in Section 9.5, during the prototyping phase very little attention will have been paid to the prototype's performance. Firstly, the performance aspect is of only minor importance in that phase, and secondly the response times are generally likely to be reasonable because of the restricted size of the database. The fact that improving a system's performance is almost inevitably at the cost of its flexibility is another reason for not being concerned about performance during the prototyping phase.

For a working system, on the other hand, it is crucial that the response times stay within acceptable limits. Increasing size of the database and numbers of users would probably soon make the prototype's performance unacceptable. So it is necessary to tune the system. Some possible ways of going about this are:

(a) *Addition of indices*. Most relational DBMSs allow the definition of indexes on (the columns of) tables. This permits direct entry to the table, so that the speed of data retrieval can be improved. The drawback of an indexed file organization is that modifying the table's contents takes longer because the indices affected also have to be updated. Whether it is worth adding an index depends on the relative frequency of read and update operations on the table.

(b) *Restructuring the database*. As explained in Section 9.2, the database structure that should be adopted during prototyping is a 1:1 projection of the normalized data model. This leads to a large number of tables or, in the case of a network DBMS, record types. To access the stored data, it will very probably be necessary to execute a large number of 'joins', or to pass through a large number of chains. Performance can thus be improved by combining tables or record types (denormalization). But again, there is a trade-off; redundant data will be stored because of the denormalization. It will therefore cost more to make changes to the database contents, since measures have to be taken to avoid inconsistencies. The utility of denormalization depends on the relative frequency with which the data will be read and updated.

(c) *Replacement of inefficient modules*. Non-procedural languages take over many development tasks from the application developer. He has only to specify the result of an action and the interpreter or compiler decides which steps are necessary to arrive at that result. However, the resulting modules are not always efficient. Particular parts of a prototype that are responsible for the slow performance of the whole have to be replaced by modules written in a more efficient third- or even a second-generation language.

2. *Security*. In a prototype, little attention is usually paid to data security. A mechanism has to be implemented which ensures that the only actions users can carry out on data are those for which, according to the specifications, they are specifically authorized. In a fourth-generation environment with an integrated data dictionary, this is often fairly simple to achieve. Thus for instance in SQL the GRANT statement can be used to assign authorizations to users for the use of tables, views, programs, etc. The authorization rules are stored in the data dictionary, which is consulted during every action on the database.

3. *Reliability*. Since speed is a particularly important factor in the realization of a prototype and the software is liable to continual change during the iterative process, there is a danger that the final prototype will be badly structured. This has repercussions on both the reliability and the maintainability of the software. The reliability can, of course, be increased by extensive testing. However, the probability of error detection diminishes with decreasing structure in the software. When the prototype is to be retained as basis for the production system, those parts that show inadequate structure must be redesigned and reprogrammed. The resulting system must then pass through the test procedures

applicable to any production system. The reliability can also be increased by a 'structured walkthrough' – a process in which the colleagues of the author of a particular piece of code are requested to deliver constructive criticism (Fagan, 1976).

10.3 CONCLUSION

The upgrading phase, and thereby the development project, is concluded when a system that complies with the entire system requirements definition, including performance and quality aspects, has been constructed and implemented in its environment. This system, including the necessary user and technical documentation, is submitted to the steering committee for approval. Before this can occur, the 'provisional design' must be updated to ensure that all modifications have been accurately documented, and that those who are to support and maintain the system have access to good design documentation.

Chapter 11

Summary of Part Two

The requirements definition phase is the most important, and at the same time the most difficult, phase of an information system development project. The correctness, unambiguity, completeness and consistency of the system requirements definition strongly determine users' reactions after system hand-over, the maintenance effort required and thus the long-term success of the project. Establishing good specifications is not a trivial matter. The traditional methods for the requirements definition phase appear to meet with patchy success. In Part Two, we have described how prototyping combines existing methods with the use of working models within a requirements definition approach characterized by iteration. This approach enables users to obtain a clearer view of their own wishes in respect of the planned system, and to communicate these wishes more clearly to the developers.

When all the activities that have to take place during the development of an information system are catalogued, it is clear that prototyping cannot be as simple as some writers on the subject would have us believe. To develop an effective system in an efficient way calls for much more than a few joint sessions at a terminal. Prototyping demands a great deal of knowledge and professionalism from those who wish to take this approach to requirements definition.

In the *project initiation* phase (Chapter 8), it must be determined whether the development of an information system really is the solution to the operational problem. If the answer is 'yes', it is necessary to decide which approach to use in the requirements definition phase. The choice between prototyping and a conventional approach depends on the characteristics of the problem situation.

How and at what point in the definition phase prototypes are used depends on aspects of the system about which uncertainty exists. In user-interface prototyping, a complete inventory is first made of the functions the system must perform, using traditional methods. Only then are prototypes used, to check how the dialogue structure and the screen or report layouts should look. However, uncertainty often affects not only the outer form of the system, but also the functionality that the system must offer the users. In functional prototyping (the kind of prototyping described in this Part), prototypes are used early in the requirements definition phase to provide a better insight into the information problem.

In the first sub-phase (*rough analysis and specification*; see Section 9.1) the provisional specifications of the planned system are drawn up. It is very important to pay sufficient attention to analyzing the problem, in order to create a stable basis for prototype design, realization and iteration. The completion of a first prototype takes place in the *design and realization* sub-phase (Section 9.2). The first activity in this sub-phase is the design and realization of a database structure. Next the functions which the information system are to perform are arranged in menus. The menu structure and some of the functions shown on the menus are implemented with the aid of CASE tools.

The activities that must take place in order to arrive at a working prototype thus differ in only a limited degree from the activities involved in developing an information system in the conventional way. This is hardly surprising: working systems do not just happen. Although a prototype does not have to satisfy the same demands as a production system and will often be incomplete in a number of aspects, it must offer sufficient functionality to enable the user to evaluate it. Even such a restricted system has to be developed step by step.

After the prototype has been built, it is submitted to the users for evaluation. In the *evaluation* sub-phase (Section 9.3), errors resulting from communication difficulties between users and developers come to light, and users have an opportunity to revise the requirements. The evaluation sub-phase may lead to the conclusion that the prototype should be modified (in the *modification* sub-phase: Section 9.4), and then re-evaluated. In that case the iterative process so characteristic of prototyping commences, and continues until the system requirements definition shows sufficient stability. To conclude the requirements definition phase, the system requirements definition is completed with performance and quality requirements. This happens in the *completion* sub-phase (described in Section 9.5).

The most important novel feature that prototyping adds to the requirements definition phase is the use of working models as a means of communication and learning. However, the goal of the definition phase is unchanged: to arrive at a complete, consistent and accurate embodiment of all the users' requirements and wishes in respect of the planned system.

At the end of the requirements definition phase there is both a system requirements definition and a prototype available. The prototype itself represents a significant investment, warranting serious consideration of whether it can be used as the basis for (part of) the production system. It will often turn out that, with relatively little effort, the prototype can be made to satisfy the demands placed on a production system. In such cases, the *upgrading* phase (see Chapter 10) is commenced, in which any necessary changes and extensions are made to the prototype.

It may be expected that a project model such as the one described here (consisting of the phases project initiation, prototyping and upgrading) will become the standard life-cycle for systems developed with contemporary CASE tools.

Part Three
CASE: The Technology Behind Prototyping

Chapter 12

Introduction to Part Three

Because prototyping is essentially a 'technology-driven' approach, it is important to understand the technology that has enabled it to mature. Only then is it possible to gauge the value of the prototyping approach, and to assess its future. Part Three describes analyst workbenches and fourth-generation development tools. As we noted in Chapter 2, these two types of tools are now widely referred to as CASE (Computer-Aided System Engineering) tools (see Section 2.3.1).

The emergence of fourth-generation tools and the advent and growing popularity of prototyping are closely related. Fourth-generation languages were in the first instance regarded and used above all as efficiency-enhancing substitutes for languages such as COBOL and PL/1. However, it soon became apparent that these languages made it possible to develop systems in a new way. Fourth-generation tools facilitate the rapid development of example systems, and therefore prototyping. So prototyping and fourth-generation technology go hand in hand.

Analyst workbenches have an equally close relationship with prototyping. We have repeatedly emphasized that the advent of prototyping does not imply that the traditional structure methods and techniques have become superfluous or obsolete. In order to use structured methods properly during the prototyping process – in which, after all, requirements definitions are repeatedly changed – it is especially desirable to have software tools to support these methods. Analyst workbenches are very valuable in projects structured along traditional lines. When a prototyping approach is followed, however, they are well-nigh indispensable.

Analyst workbenches are starting to include prototyping facilities such as screen painters, report writers and dialogue managers. Sometimes these facilities are closely coupled to the other components of the workbench. Such workbenches clearly visualize the relationship between prototypes and structured methods and techniques. Some are closely coupled to a fourth-generation development environment or program generator, which again facilitates the combined use of prototypes and diagramming techniques to model a system.

Since the data dictionary takes a central role in all CASE tools, in Chapter 13 we first explain some basic concepts of data dictionary systems (DDSs). Chapter 14 discusses analyst workbenches; this chapter goes some way beyond the things the reader has to know about analyst workbenches to assess their relationship with prototyping. We have chosen this approach in order to make the chapter also useful as a frame of reference during the evaluation and selection of a workbench. Chapter 15 discusses fourth-generation languages and fourth-generation development environments. Finally, in Chapter 16 we comment on the 'state of the art' in the CASE area.

Chapter 13

Basic Concepts of Data Dictionary Systems

13.1 HISTORY

Most of the major suppliers of fourth-generation software (such as Cullinet, Software AG and CINCOM) proclaim that the data dictionary is central to the architecture of their proprietary products. It has not always received such profuse attention from that direction. In the recent past, suppliers and purchasers of fourth-generation software paid much more heed to the quality of the underlying DBMS than to the capacities – or even the availability – of a data dictionary. The increased interest in the latter is primarily a consequence of the growing popularity of data-driven development approaches, but also of the increase in the number of components of the various fourth-generation environments and the concomitant problems of integrating these components. The data dictionary can perform an exceptionally useful function in this area.

Although the data dictionary has only recently become the centre of interest, it has been in existence for some time. Its origin lies in the idea that information is just as important to an organization as other operating resources and consequently, like other resources, has to be managed. The person responsible for this task in an organization is known as the 'data administrator'. A DDS is the most important tool of the data administrator, who uses it to store data about that for which he is responsible: data. Data about data is generally referred to as 'meta-data'.[1] Examples are: the precise meaning, an informal description and the owner of a specific item of data. A data dictionary – the 'heart' of a DDS – is simply a database containing meta-data.

Since the appearance of DDSs, there has been much discussion about the role they should play in the development process. Traditionally, a data dictionary is used to store meta-data about the data held in various databases and about the relationships among these data. Sometimes it also contains meta-data about the structure of the applications that make use of these databases, the screens that form part of an application, etc. All the components of an application, the databases which these components utilize and the connections between the various parts of the system are then documented in the data dictionary. In such cases the DDS is almost indispensable during the realization and maintenance phases.

More recently, the data dictionary has been used as an aid in earlier phases of the development process. Sometimes called the 'encyclopedia' or 'system encyclopedia', it is then also the central point for storage of all the meta-data resulting from the

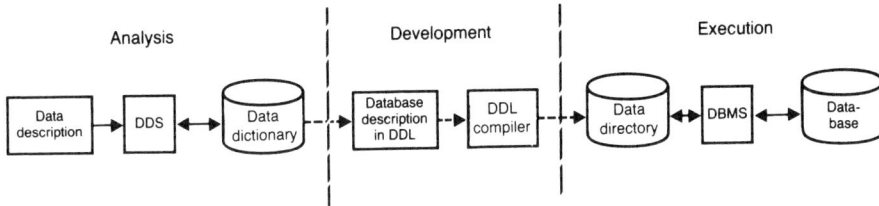

Figure 13.1 Relationship between a passive DDS and the DBMS.

analysis and design process. The data dictionary has gradually evolved from a tool aimed purely at the data administrator to one which provides support in practically all the activities that take place during planning, development and maintenance of information systems.

13.2 ACTIVE AND PASSIVE DATA DICTIONARY SYSTEMS

There are two kinds of DDS: *passive* and *active* (or *dynamic*). The first DDSs were of the passive type. A passive data dictionary is not consulted by the DBMS (for example to locate the data requested by an application program). For this purpose the DBMS uses its own source of meta-data: the data directory. The data directory is filled by making a description of the database structure in the data description language (DDL) of the DBMS, and then submitting this description to the DDL compiler. With a passive DDS, the description is first stored in the data dictionary; from here the database structure description in the appropriate DDL is subsequently generated from the data dictionary contents (Fig. 13.1).

Information about data elements, data structures and other system components is thus maintained separately from the databases and the applications that this information describes. It will be clear that in this case very strict procedures must be set up to keep the contents of the data dictionary correct and up to date. Updating the data dictionary is time consuming, and developers often see it as an irritating chore that slows the progress of the project. Thus when there is a possibility for them to by-pass the data dictionary, they will be inclined to do so. In that situation, the DDS ceases to represent reality, and thus loses credibility.

An active DDS, in contrast to its passive counterpart, is closely integrated with a DBMS. Active data dictionaries satisfy a directory function in addition to a dictionary one: the DBMS consults such a dictionary at run-time for the necessary data definitions, validation rules, etc. (see Fig. 13.2). The DBMS relies entirely on the data dictionary/directory for its meta-data and does not use any internal directories of its own. The database structure can therefore be modified only by changing the data dictionary contents. As a consequence, an active DDS always provides the user with an up to date, complete and accurate image of the database. The updating of an active data dictionary is a natural part of the development process; and the developer cannot by-pass it.

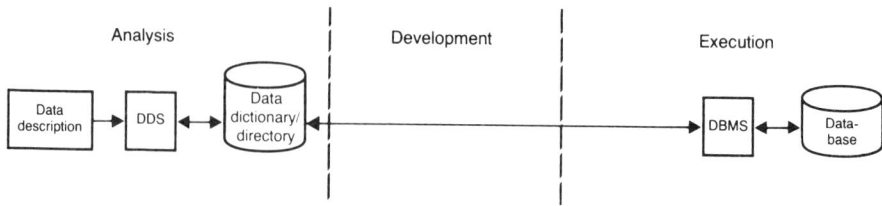

Figure 13.2 Relationship between an active DDS and the DBMS.

As well as 'active' or 'dynamic', the term *'integrated'* is also commonly used in connection with DDSs in a fourth-generation environment. It indicates that every component of that environment (such as a screen painter or a report writer) uses the data dictionary as a central storage place for all input and output. The individual tools communicate with one another via it. Everything created during the development process is directly accessible from each component of the development environment. When the developer alters the 'picture' or the 'edit rule' of a field, for instance, all screens on which the field appears will immediately make use of the changed definition. Changes in the structure of programs, or in the way programs make use of the database, are immediately reflected in the data dictionary. The latter is thus updated both directly by the developer and by the various components of the fourth-generation environment. Since the data dictionary continually contains an up-to-date image of the various system components and of the links among them, the developer can quickly establish what the consequences of a change made to a particular system component will be.

An active and integrated DDS thus offers considerable advantages over a passive one. It is automatically updated when changes are made to the application, while a passive DDS has to be continually updated by the developer. The DDS is an integral part of the development environment, so the developer can easily and quickly obtain access to it. Active data dictionaries demand far less attention and effort on the developer's part than do passive ones, and provide a much better support during the realization of an application.

However, active DDSs do also have some disadvantages. Firstly, they are generally so closely attuned to the needs of the related DBMS that the data dictionary is not usable by other DBMSs. In a situation where more than one DBMS is used – as is the case in most organizations of any size – it is necessary to resort to an independent (and thus passive) DDS from which the DDL can be generated for multiple DBMSs. Another problem linked with active DDSs is the negative influence on performance caused by frequent consultation of a large data dictionary by the DBMS.

13.3 THE STRUCTURE OF A DATA DICTIONARY

One of the principal characteristics of a DDS is the structure of the data dictionary that forms the heart of such a system. The various DDSs that are presently available display very large differences both in the data dictionary structure provided by the supplier and in the possibilities that the DDS offers for modifying or extending this structure. It may be necessary to modify or expand the data dictionary structure in order to adapt a DDS to the requirements of a specific organization, for example in respect of the development methods to be supported.

An active DDS is, as stated, closely integrated with a specific DBMS. The structure of such a dictionary is therefore completely attuned to the needs of the associated DBMS. If, for instance, the DBMS recognizes the concepts 'file' and 'segment', the data dictionary will make it possible to store meta-data concerning files and segments. The user of the DDS cannot modify this data dictionary structure, since the DBMS then will obviously no longer function. Extension of the structure of such data dictionaries is, in general, poorly supported. There is no good reason why this should be so; many suppliers of data dictionaries have so far simply failed to react to the need for extensibility. They regard the DDS purely as an adjunct to the DBMS.

Passive data dictionaries also usually have a default structure implemented by the supplier, which is usually DBMS independent. When it has been decided to make use of a specific DBMS a description is generated, in terms that are understandable to that DBMS, from the description of the database structure that is stored in the dictionary in DBMS-independent terms. Because the suppliers of passive DDSs do not think in terms of the needs of a specific DBMS but of an organization's needs in the area of data management, in most cases these DDSs allow their users to change the default structure. Extensibility can be realized in two different ways. Firstly, the DDS supplier can predefine a number of extensions to the data dictionary and offer them to users as options. A second approach offers much more flexibility; here the supplier gives DDS users a facility for defining new meta-data types and the relations between them.

NOTE

1. The term 'meta-data' is used in this publication to indicate not only data about data, but also all other kinds of data that are produced during the analysis, design and implementation phases (descriptions of activities in the organization, descriptions of software and so on).

Chapter 14

Analyst Workbenches

We have already repeatedly emphasized that during prototyping, just as during the conventional linear process, structured development methods and techniques continue to be intensively used. With the aid of these methods, the problem can be divided into comprehensible and manageable pieces and the results of the analysis and design work can be documented. Developers can use the diagrams, formal textual descriptions and informal descriptions that are produced as a means of communication with one another.

When using structured methods and techniques, the developer is faced with the problem of maintaining the resulting documentation. Early in the development process, the information needs of users have not stabilized. Continual revision of the diagrams, texts, lists and tables that are produced is exceptionally time consuming. In particular, modifying diagrams using an eraser, pencil and template demands a great deal of effort.

Besides the redrawing of diagrams, much effort is required to keep the various analysis and design data consistent. Many links, sometimes complex ones, exist among the documents which a developer produces. Redundant information is often (deliberately) included, for example in overviews that give the developer the opportunity to study the system from various angles. Thus, the same data flow may be found in a number of different dataflow diagrams, in matrices bringing activities and data flows into relation with one another, in lists giving an overview of all data flows per diagram and in tables showing the elements of which the various data flows are composed. When making alterations, it is practically impossible to avoid missing some point or other, thereby introducing inconsistency. This is particularly true when the project is large and/or complex.

Inconsistencies and deficiencies may also occur when the developer forgets to check whether all the rules imposed by the methodology on the development process, and on the products resulting from that process, have been obeyed. A good method has a large number of rules. For instance, in the 'tree' of diagrams produced during top-down activity analysis, there will generally be a rule that all information serving as input to a specific activity must also be an input in the diagram forming the decomposition of that activity. This rule ensures that nothing gets accidentally lost in the decomposition process. As well as rules for the decomposition process, diagramming techniques impose rules for the way in which diagrams must be constructed. For instance, there will be restrictions on the types of object which may be connected by flows. Considering the number of such rules, there is a real danger that the developer will overlook one. In practice, the rules may not all be known explicitly, or the method may give no indication of which rules may potentially be contravened by a particular action of the developer. The developer thus does not know what to check, and when.

Certainly, when an information problem of some scale is involved, using structured methods is so time consuming that correct application of the method threatens to claim the most attention, as opposed to analysis of the problem situation and the designing of solutions for it. There is then a danger that the project will drown, as it were, in a sea of paper. This kind of situation can be prevented by making use of an analyst workbench – an integrated set of automated tools supporting the developer in the use of structured methods and techniques. Without analyst workbenches, it is almost impossible to use such methods properly in a practical situation. This applies even more when these methods are used during the prototyping process, in which speed is of the essence and the information needs are prone to rapid change.

Section 14.1 describes, in some detail, which components should be present in an analyst workbench, and the requirements that those components must meet. This blueprint of the ideal analyst workbench can serve as a frame of reference during the process of evaluation and selection of a workbench. Section 14.2. contains a classification of automated tools for the information analyst and systems designer.

14.1 ARCHITECTURE OF AN ANALYST WORKBENCH

As stated in Chapter 2, in an ideal case an analyst workbench forms part of a larger set of tools that supports not only the analyst and designer, but everyone involved in information systems engineering (information planning, systems development and systems maintenance). In that chapter we referred to this more extensive set of tools as an ISEE – an Integrated Systems Engineering Environment. Figure 14.1 illustrates the architecture of an ISEE and the place of the analyst workbench without this architecture.

The 'heart' of an ISEE, and thus also of an analyst workbench, is formed by a data dictionary which stores all the meta-data (or, synonymously, 'development data') produced during the development process. This data dictionary is described in detail in Section 14.1.1. Around it is arranged a number of facilities which provide support for the various activities of the information analyst and the system designer. The following must be present:

1. A diagram editor.
2. (Intelligent) text editors.
3. Prototyping facilities.
4. Facilities for analyzing the completeness and consistency of the dictionary contents.
5. Facilities for automation of particular analysis and design tasks.
6. Facilities for reporting on the dictionary contents.

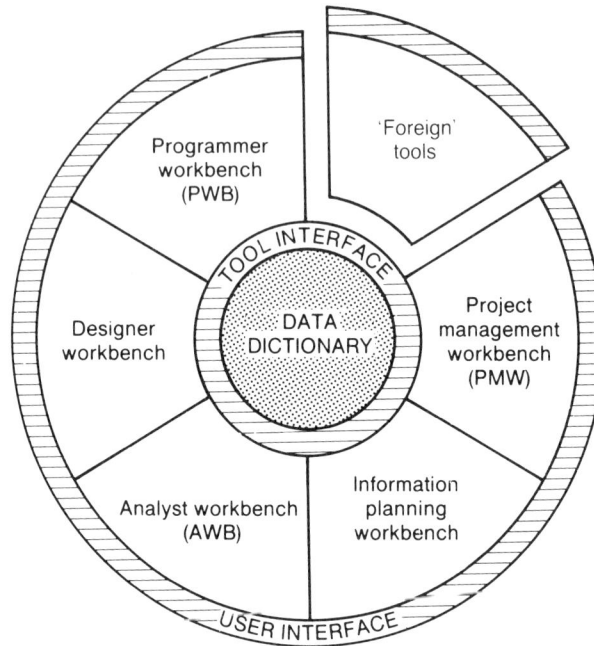

Figure 14.1 Architecture of an ISEE.

7. Facilities to allow for the shared use of meta-data between developers.
8. Facilities that support the users in following the steps prescribed by the method.

These facilities are discussed in Sections 14.1.2–9 inclusive. The user of a workbench communicates with all the tools via a single interface, so that the whole has a uniform appearance. This interface is discussed in Section 14.1.10. The other components of an ISEE are summarized in Section 14.1.11, which also considers briefly the relation between these and the analyst workbench. Finally, Section 14.1.12 describes a few other points requiring attention during appraisal of a workbench.

14.1.1 The data dictionary

An analyst workbench must make it possible for the developer to store all data produced during the development process. Developers of analyst workbenches generally call this central store of meta-data a 'data dictionary' (see Section 13.1). Another term which the reader may encounter in the literature is '*(system) encyclopedia*'. However, these terms are rarely used by IPSE developers; they generally call this central repository a '*design database*' or '*project database*', and its contents '*design data*' or *development data*'. In this book, we shall use the term 'data dictionary'. The terms 'meta-data' and 'development data' will be treated as interchangeable.

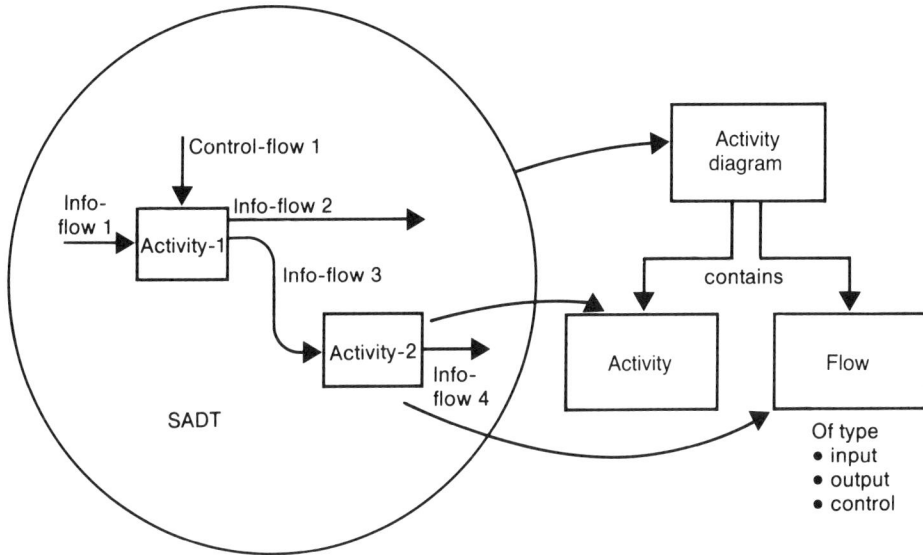

Figure 14.2 Dictionary structure as a derivative of the supported method.

The structure of the data dictionary derives directly from the methods supported. By way of illustration, Fig. 14.2 shows a dictionary structure which could be adopted for storing SADT activity diagrams. If the method distinguishes the meta-data type 'activity', for example, the data dictionary should make it possible to store meta-data of this type (such as 'order processing' or 'invoicing'). By storing all the development data centrally and only once, it becomes easier to ensure consistency and completeness – besides saving the developer the effort of repeated data entry.

An analyst workbench should include adequate facilities for system configuration management. It must be possible to retain different versions of the same development data in the data dictionary. It must also be possible to go back to an earlier version of a particular item, or even to a previous version of an entire model, after a modification has been made. In addition the workbench must have a status management facility. It must be possible to allocate a different status to each version of development data and to sets of development data. Configuration management facilities are particularly important during prototyping. It is almost impossible to keep track of all changes and versions of models and associated prototypes by hand.

14.1.2 The diagram editor

An analyst workbench should support all the diagramming techniques associated with a specific methodology. The tool should make it possible to construct, save and modify diagrams in an interactive and user-friendly way.

OPERATIONS ON THE DIAGRAMS

At the very least, basic operations such as adding, removing and repositioning objects in diagrams, and the connection of objects, must be available. When objects are connected, it is useful if the tool prevents the connecting lines from passing through objects in the diagram. It must be possible to minimize the number of intersecting lines automatically, and when intersections are unavoidable there must be no ambiguity about which objects are actually linked together. During repositioning of an object, any connections with other objects must be preserved. The best way of repositioning is known as '*dragging*' – here the object remains visible during repositioning. A less sophisticated method of repositioning consists of first pointing to the object to be moved, and then pointing to the new position. It is more difficult to position the moved object accurately in this way. If the diagramming technique forbids open-ended connections, all associated connections must be removed when an object is deleted. It is particularly useful to have a facility for deleting or repositioning groups of objects in a single operation.

When a diagram includes a large number of objects, there should be a facility for '*zooming in*' (enlarging a selected part of the diagram). The indicated portion of the diagram can then be enlarged to occupy the whole screen. It must be possible to repeat this a number of times. Naturally, it must also be possible to go back to a previous '*zoom level*', and to display the diagram again in its entirety. The tool must also show which part of a diagram is on the screen. Finally, it is useful if the workbench has a facility for automatically selecting the zoom level required for the diagram to fill the whole screen.

If the diagram technique includes the possibility of describing an object in greater detail in a new diagram (*decomposition*), the automated tool should make it possible for the developer to jump from one level of detail to another (to '*explode*' and '*implode*' the diagram). Some methods provide for the possibility of describing an object in greater detail from various viewpoints. In this case it must be possible to select from a number of types of diagram during 'explosion'.

DIAGRAM STORAGE

As explained in the last section, the dictionary of an analyst workbench contains all the data produced during the analysis and design process. Diagrams can be regarded as providing a graphic 'window' on the contents of the dictionary. They constitute the view that the developer chooses to take of the dictionary's contents, and the medium which the developer wishes to use for manipulating these contents.

Diagrams must, therefore, be an accurate representation of what is present in the dictionary at all times. The simplest way of preventing diagrams and data dictionary contents from getting out of step is to store only the contents of a diagram, and not the diagram itself. The latter must then always be regenerated from the latest dictionary contents. In this, the workbench must take account of the developer's requirements in the respect of the layout: if a developer has departed from the default layout, the workbench must be able to regenerate it unchanged.

ACCESS TO THE DATA DICTIONARY

In general, diagrams do not make it possible to represent everything the developer might wish to record about the various objects. Simple examples of development data with no graphic equivalents are synonyms and informal descriptions. A workbench should therefore provide the developer with direct access to the data dictionary, so that the information system under development can be described in more detail than is possible by diagrams alone. The workbench should also provide the developer with good text-editing facilities for this purpose.

Developers will usually wish to use the diagram editor to sketch the broad outlines of the problem situation, and then to add more detail to the resulting entries in the data dictionary. However, some developers may adopt the opposite approach – first entering a complete textual description and then producing diagrams. A good workbench must make both approaches possible, and also the instant switching between diagram editing and more detailed description of the various objects in the data dictionary.

14.1.3 (Intelligent) text editors

Graphic languages become inadequate when the amount of detail needed to describe something reaches a certain level. For example, complex integrity rules can be represented with only the greatest difficulty, or perhaps not at all, in diagrammatic form. In the INFOMOD information-modeling method (Jardine and Griethuysen, 1987a,b), diagrams are used only to provide a fairly crude sketch of an information structure (the INFOMOD equivalent of an entity-relationship model); as soon as it becomes necessary to describe more complex matters, INFOMOD provides a formal language (based on predicate logic). Similar examples can also be found in the design and realization phases. To describe the component modules of the information system in any detail, it soon becomes necessary to use pseudocode; for writing programs, a programming language is used.

Strict language rules apply to INFOMOD models, to pseudocode and to programs. Only specified language elements and constructions are permitted. For each language associated with the supported methodology, the workbench must provide an 'intelligent' text editor (one that 'knows' the language). The developer must be allowed to use only permitted language constructions, and must receive clear warning when the grammar has been contravened. Intelligent text editors of this kind are sometimes called 'syntax directed'.

When a workbench supports languages, the text and the contents of the data dictionary must remain in agreement. For example, in a pseudocode module description, reference will often be made to data elements which are defined elsewhere in the data dictionary. If the name of such a data element is changed, the change must also be made to the pseudocode. The workbench must see the data element names in the pseudocode not as mere text, but must also know that the code refers at that point to a defined data element.

Like diagrams, text such as a written information model can be regarded as providing one particular 'window' on the dictionary contents. This permits the developer to see and manipulate the dictionary contents while using the most suitable medium for the task at hand. As with diagrams, the workbench should not store texts separately from the dictionary data but rather should regenerate a text as and when the developer needs it. This makes it possible to prevent conflicts between the text and the dictionary. When regenerating text from the data dictionary, the workbench must 'remember' the layout the developer has chosen.

14.1.4 Prototyping facilities

Generally, an analyst workbench should support different approaches to requirements definition, including prototyping. For describing a dialogue structure, the developer uses the diagramming techniques of the method being followed, and hence the diagram editor (see Section 14.1.2). However, this will not support screen and report definitions, since these are not diagrams. Therefore an analyst workbench must also be equipped with a screen painter and a report writer.

On the basis of the design of the dialogue, screens and reports, the workbench must be able to generate a prototype that mimics the user interface. It is particularly useful if such a prototype can run independently of the workbench, so that users can test it without needing a copy of the workbench itself. In order to support functional prototyping also, the workbench has either to include a relational DBMS and a fourth-generation language, or to be closely coupled to a fourth-generation environment containing such facilities.

In screen and report definitions, data elements which have already been defined in the dictionary will be re-used. The workbench must ensure that no conflicts arise between the screen or report, on the one hand, and the contents of the data dictionary, on the other. If, for example, the length of a data element is changed, the workbench must indicate which screens and reports have to be modified. Furthermore, it must ensure that the diagrammatic description of the system does not contradict the prototype model of the system. If, for instance, an entity-relationship diagram is changed, the database structure of the prototype has to be changed accordingly, or the workbench has to point out possible inconsistencies.

14.1.5 Analysis facilities

The strength of a development method lies particularly in the rules, or *constraints*, which it imposes on the products resulting from the development process. Rules for diagrams, central to most methods, can be divided into a number of classes, for example:

1. *Rules that apply to a single object in a single diagram.* An example of such a rule that might apply in a specific method is: 'a data flow in a dataflow diagram must always have a unique name'.

2. *Rules that apply to a number of objects in a single diagram.* An example of a rule of this class is: 'a process in a dataflow diagram must have at least one data flow as input and at least one data flow as output'. Another commonly occurring rule is: 'objects of type *X* and objects of type *Y* may not be connected'.
3. *Rules that apply to objects in different diagrams of the same type.* An example of such a rule is: 'all data output from a process must also be output from the diagram which represents the decomposition of that process'.
4. *Rules that apply to objects in diagrams of differing types.* An example of a rule of this class is: 'each of the entity types about which processes exchange data through data flows must occur in an entity-relationship diagram'.

The contents of the data dictionary will ultimately have to satisfy all these rules. However, many constraints do not have to be satisfied immediately; some constraints are always violated in the first instance. An example of a rule of this kind is that every process in a dataflow diagram must have at least one data flow as input. At the moment that the information analyst draws a process this will not be the case. Another example is provided by rules applying to a number of mutually related diagrams. At the moment that one of these diagrams is modified, there is a possibility that the rules will be violated. One can hardly insist that the developer instantly rectifies these inconsistencies, since a considerable amount of work is associated with such corrections.

A workbench must therefore support the developer in tracing the inevitable conflicts and deficiencies, whenever the developer thinks it is desirable or useful. Thus it is he who decides when the various rules must be satisfied. This also applies to those rules which in principle could be enforced immediately (such as 'every object in a diagram must have a description'). A workbench must offer support at times when the developer is still working in a sketchy and exploratory way, and is not yet interested in being complete and consistent. This will be particularly so when prototyping.

Although the graphics capabilities of a workbench are generally impressive, and are often the main motive for acquisition, its real strength is to be found in its analysis facilities.

14.1.6 Generation facilities

Some parts of the development process are sufficiently well understood to be formalized, and thus automated. This applies to the programming activity, for example, illustrated by the growth of fourth-generation languages and program generators. In the analysis and design phases, too, some activities are so well understood that they can be written down as algorithms.

This can occur, for example, when an activity in a diagram is renumbered. Diagrams originating from decomposition of the renumbered activity, and activities in these lower level diagrams, can be renumbered automatically. Another example is generating a normalized database schema on the basis of a specification of entity types, attribute types and the functional dependencies among them.

A final example is the generation of a module structure chart on the basis of a

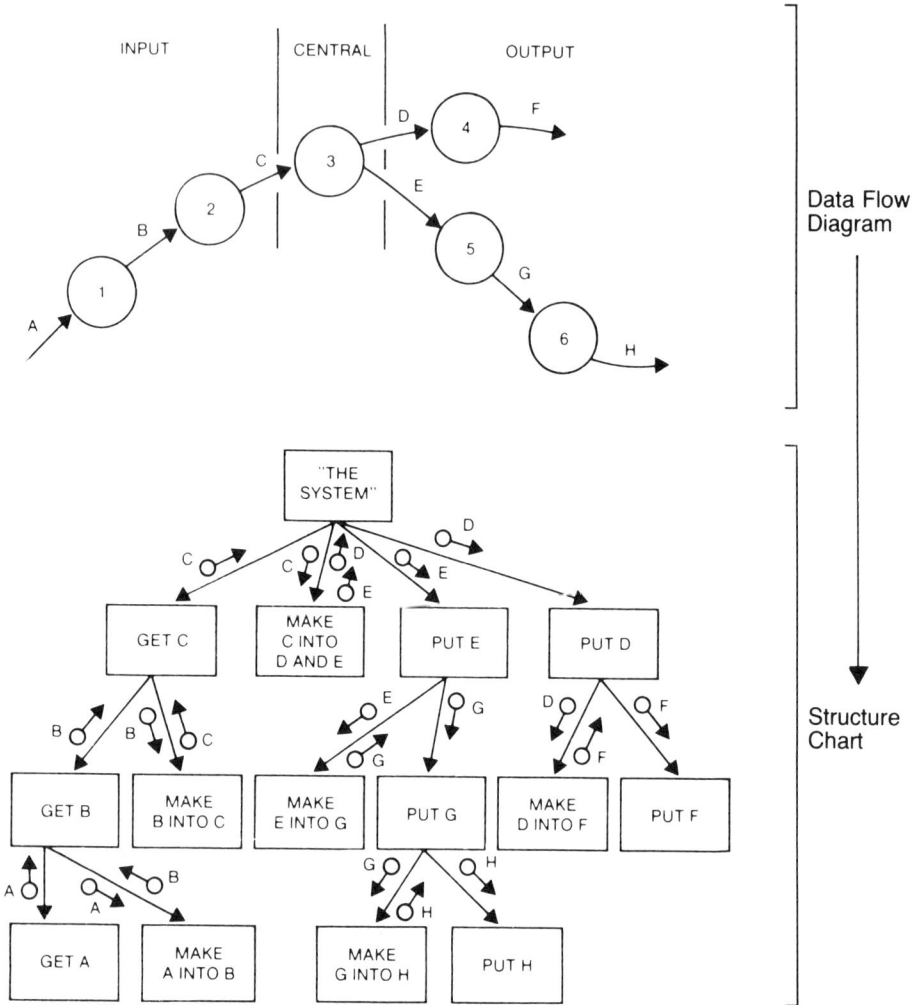

Figure 14.3 Structure chart generation on the basis of a dataflow diagram. (*Source:* Adapted from DeMarco (1978). Reprinted with permission.)

dataflow diagram (see Fig. 14.3). The transformation of the dataflow diagram into a first-cut structure chart is fairly mechanical and can therefore be automated. Although this does not usually result immediately in an optimal module structure, it is possible to generate a first proposal. Obviously, a tool must not leave it to the developer to produce a structure chart unaided, and then merely indicate potential conflicts between the structure chart and the dataflow diagram.

14.1.7 Facilities for report generation

During the development process, the developer will wish to generate *ad hoc* reports on the contents of the data dictionary. A summary of all diagrams which have undergone changes since a certain date, or summaries of data which have been changed by a certain process, are examples of such reports. For this purpose, the developer must have access to a query language – preferably a non-procedural one like SQL – and a facility for modifying the lay-out of generated reports according to taste. The analyst workbench must offer the developer the possibility to save report structures so that they can be re-executed at a later date.

At pre-arranged times, the project team will have to communicate with the various parties involved (client, steering group, users, etc.) about the results achieved. It is then often necessary to produce a document containing the requested information (for instance, a system requirements definition). A workbench must offer desk-top publishing facilities for producing documents of this kind, which will generally include both graphics (diagrams) and text (introductory text, reports on data dictionary contents, etc.). It must be possible to use headers and footers, to produce indexes, lists, etc.

14.1.8 Facilities for the shared use of meta-data

In a great many cases, the analysis and design data produced by a developer are also of interest to other members of the project team. Examples of this are information models and project-specific data-element definitions. Moreover, a developer will wish to (or will have to) make use of pre-existing development data, originating from sources external to the project. Examples here are activity and information models that the developer can use as a starting point for his own analysis activities. A workbench must include facilities which make it possible to share development data. Re-usability is particularly important during prototyping.

In order to share development data with others, each developer must be able to use the same 'logical' data dictionary. In principle, this can be technically realized in a number of ways. The workbench can comprise a single physical data dictionary on a minicomputer or a mainframe, which gives various developers access to this data dictionary, preferably at the same time. When the workbench is also required to offer good graphics facilities and a user-friendly user interface, it will be necessary to use a personal computer or intelligent workstation. To achieve acceptable response times in these circumstances, the locally needed meta data will often have to be locally stored. Thus the workbench must also have its own ('local') data dictionary. Examples of adequate technical architectures in a situation where development data are shared with other people in the organization are:

1. A *star network*, with a central data dictionary in which all data of interest to more than one person are stored.
2. A *local area network* (*LAN*), with a number of local dictionaries and a project dictionary, in which all data of interest to more than one project team member

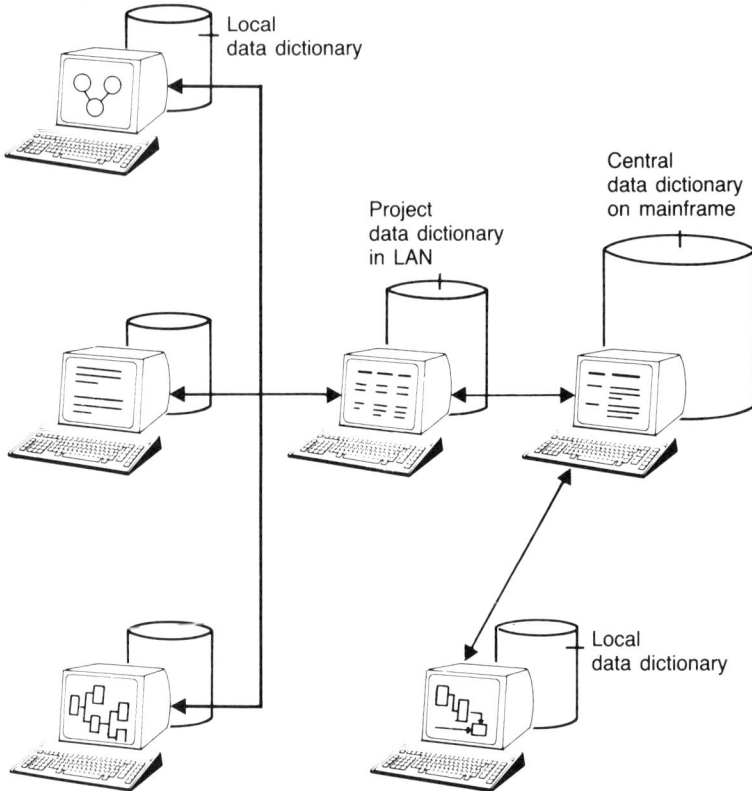

Figure 14.4 Technical architecture.

are stored, coupled to a central dictionary on the mainframe, in which all development data of interest to more than one project are stored.

3. A combination of the above two architectures (see Fig. 14.4).

It will be clear that prevention of conflicts between the development data in the various dictionaries is complex. A workbench must provide the necessary facilities in this area including: facilities for 'locking' development data transported to another dictionary for update, facilities for recording who has obtained what development data at what time and good status management facilities.

The developer should desirably be concerned as little as possible with how the development data are distributed among the various data dictionaries. When he needs a particular item of development data, the workbench should determine where that item is located, and should automatically arrange the transfer of that item of development data from one dictionary to another. The distribution should be as transparent as possible to the developer. Of course the workbench should include security facilities to ensure that developers have access only to development data that they are authorized to use.

14.1.9 Navigator facility

So far we have only discussed the support a workbench must offer for creating, modifying and keeping consistent the products that a developer has to produce according to the method supported. A method also defines the order in which the various development activities must be carried out; for example, it may prescribe that the following procedure should be adhered to in the system requirements definition phase:

1. Create an activity model.
2. Create an entity-relationship model for each activity.
3. Merge the separate entity-relationship models.
4. Check whether there are conflicts between the consolidated entity-relationship model and the activity model.
5. Decompose each activity in a new activity model and return to step 2, or if the lowest level of decomposition has been reached then stop.

A workbench must offer support in this area. It will have to include a navigator facility which takes the developer by the hand and leads him through the development process. After each activity, he should automatically be confronted with either the next task to be done or a list of tasks from which a choice must be made. As he builds up experience with the method, he will probably wish to take a few liberties; the strictly prescribed sequence of activities will start to feel like a straitjacket. It must, therefore, be possible to inactivate the navigator component of the workbench.

14.1.10 User interface

It is obviously desirable that all workbench components communicate with the developer in a uniform way. This can best be realized by handling all communication between the tools and the developer through one and the same interface.

INTERACTION MECHANISM

In constructing and editing diagrams, it is often necessary to use commands with positional information (coordinates). A good interaction mechanism minimizes the number of times that the developer has to switch from one input medium to another. In this case, a suitable interaction mechanism is the *'mouse'*, in combination with menus. The mouse is used both for selecting a required action from a menu (such as 'add object'), and for indicating the place or object(s) to which the action refers. The keyboard is then needed only for entering text. Obviously, the mouse/menu combination works smoothly only when the response times are very low; a menu must appear on the screen as soon as it is asked for. Going through a series of nested menus must not take longer than typing in a command.

TYPES OF MENU

Nowadays there is a choice of several types of menu. *Pop-up menus* appear on demand at the cursor position on the screen; *roll-down menus* appear when the cursor is positioned on a bar at the top of the screen, and the menu 'rolls down' rather like a window blind; *static menus* have a fixed position on the screen and are always visible. Each of these types has its own merits in specific cases. A menu may have fixed contents, but it may instead show only those actions permitted in the current circumstances ('*context-dependent*' *menus*). In this case, the actions which are not permitted at the time the menu is invoked should not be completely erased from the menu, since the developer must then always search through the menu for the position of the required action. In this situation it is better if the 'inactive' and 'active' actions are distinguished by some means, for example by giving them different colours or displaying the inactive choices less distinctly than the active ones.

WINDOWING

Ideally a workbench should have a '*windowing*' facility. This makes it possible for the developer to use more than one of the facilities described earlier at the same time. For example, he could edit a diagram in one window, while a report which is needed for this is displayed in a second, or he could run a prototype and at the same time study the consequences of a change to a state transition diagram on it. Ideally, there should be '*true multi-tasking*', where the tasks which must be carried out in the various windows proceed simultaneously. This makes it possible, for example, to perform a time-consuming analysis of the data dictionary in one window while editing a diagram in another. When modification to one diagram means that other diagrams (whether visible or not) also have to be modified, this should happen immediately.

USE OF COLOR

Effective use of color should be made within a workbench. For example, different types of diagram can be given different colors, or matters where attention is still required can be distinguished from those which have already been dealt with by use of different colors. However, colors must not be used for mere effect. Bright, spectacular color combinations look attractive at first but soon become irritating in continued use.

14.1.11 Interfaces to other tools

During the requirements definition phase, the information analyst uses the results of the information-planning phase. The technical designer then designs a system that complies with all the defined requirements. The technical design is input to the realization phase, in which the system is actually constructed. The whole process of developing software can thus be seen as an ordered series of transformations. There are strong relationships among the products of the various phases. Obviously, there is also a close relationship between the development and the project management processes.

An important criterion in appraising analyst workbenches is, therefore, the extent to which the tool is coupled with tools for other activities which take place before, during and after the project. In the ideal case, the analyst workbench forms an integral part of an ISEE. There should be interfaces to the tools for the information-planning process, for the realization phase, for the maintenance phase and for project management. The separate tools must communicate with one another via the data dictionary, so that the relationships among the development data produced in the various phases can be preserved. The coupling among tools is realized through the data dictionary, and not through interfaces among the separate components of the ISEE.

INFORMATION-PLANNING TOOLS

The tools needed for the information-planning activity are broadly similar to the facilities that must be present in an analyst workbench. For example, diagrams are also used here. However, the information planner does not need (or hardly needs) intelligent text editors and facilities for screen and report definition such as are required in an analyst workbench. Generally these facilities are used to describe a system in more detail than is needed in the information-planning phase. During information planning, extensive use is made of matrices to visualize relationships among development data (such as functions and entity-types). A workbench for the information planner must therefore comprise good facilities for matrix handling.

Information planning ultimately results in, among other things, the demarcation of a number of projects. This is where the interface with the analyst workbench lies: the activities and entity types identified at a high level of abstraction in the information-planning phase are the starting point for further analysis of the problem.

PROGRAMMING AIDS

There are a large number of program generators, particularly in the sector of business information systems, but also in the technical area. Desirably, there should at least be interfaces between the analyst workbench and generators of this kind, so that (parts of) applications can be generated automatically. This is, of course, particularly important during prototyping. In general, however, only relatively simple applications can be realized in this way. To be able to construct more complex applications and prototypes, the workbench must be closely coupled to a fourth-generation development environment. Chapter 15 discusses fourth-generation languages and development environments.

MAINTENANCE TOOLS

During the maintenance phase, maintenance staff will primarily use the same methods and techniques as are utilized during the analysis, design and programming phases. If a structured approach is followed, any changes that users ask for will first lead to a change in the system requirements definition. Then the links that the developer (and the analyst workbench) know to exist between the system requirements definition and the technical design are used to trace any consequences for the technical design. The same is done to determine which (parts of) programs have to be changed. In a growing number of cases, this last step (and perhaps even the preceding one) will no

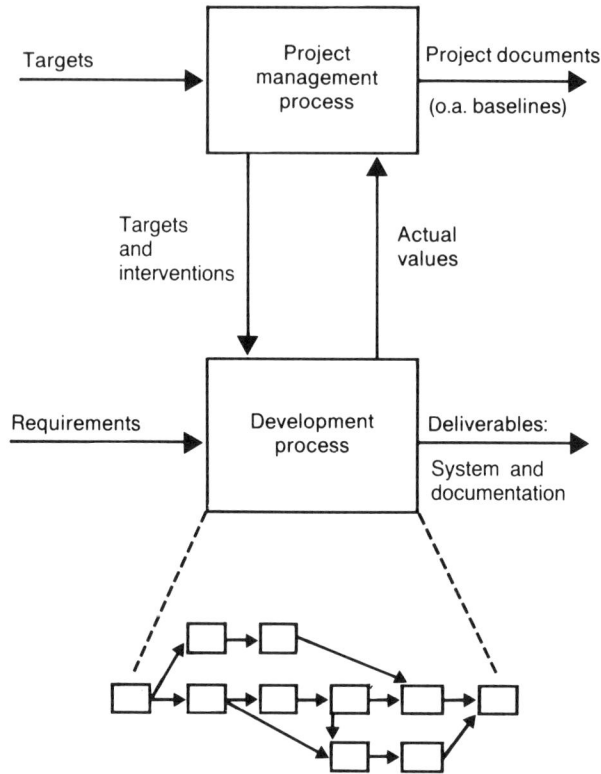

Figure 14.5 Relationship between the development process and the management process.

longer be necessary: the modified system will simply be regenerated on the basis of the system requirements definition.

PROJECT MANAGEMENT TOOLS

The project manager controls the development process by dividing it into small, comprehensible units of work, by continually checking how far the well-defined aim of such a unit has been realized and by taking corrective action in the event of deviations from the plan (see Fig. 14.5).

During the set-up of a project, a 'project management workbench' must give the project leader the choice of a number of project models (describing the activities and products for various types of project). Ideally, the tool supports him in making a selection. He must be able to adapt the selected model to the local problem situation. Next, the various tasks must be allocated to the respective developers. Here it must be possible to take into account the maximum time that the developers have available for the project in the various periods that it will occupy. A time and cost plan can be drawn up on this basis. When the developer uses his own workbench, he should be automatically confronted with the tasks to be carried out. The project model and the task allocation chosen by the project leader must thus form the initial input for the navigator (see Section 14.1.10). When a developer concludes a piece of work, this should be made known to the project management workbench. When the actual situation deviates from the time, cost and capacity plans, the project management workbench should draw this to the project leader's attention, and a new plan must be automatically generated.

'OPEN' ARCHITECTURE

In some situations, more facilities will be needed than are offered by the ISEE or analyst workbench. A workbench must therefore make it possible to use development aids acquired from other sources, and must include facilities for extending its functionality. The data dictionary must be accessible to these add-on facilities, and it must be possible for them to function under the standard man/machine interface of the workbench. A workbench which makes allowance for add-on tools has an 'open' architecture.

To allow the addition of third-party tools, there must be well-defined and preferably standard interfaces to both the software that handles the dialogue with the workbench user (the window manager, dialogue manager, etc.) and the data dictionary. Standard interfaces of this kind are currently under development. Within ESPRIT (a European program for stimulating research in the field of information technology), there is work proceeding on a 'Portable Common Tools Environment' (PCTE) project (Commission of the European Communities, 1986; Lyons, 1986). This project (in which Bull, GEC, ICL, Nixdorf, Olivetti and Siemens are participating) has already resulted in a first working version of a PCTE, and in a commercially available implementation (Emeraude from GIE-Emeraude). The PCTE specification will in all probability also be adopted by national research and development projects of the various countries participating in ESPRIT (for example the Alvey project in the UK).

14.1.12 Miscellaneous criteria

There are of course criteria other than those discussed in the preceding sections which must be taken into account in appraising and selecting a workbench. The most important of these are summarized as follows:

1. *Security*. A workbench must comprise facilities for ensuring that only authorized persons can inspect, add, modify or delete data.
2. *Back-up and recovery*. In the ideal case a workbench makes frequent back-ups automatically. There should at least be an easily used facility for backing up (parts of) a project.
3. *Performance*. A workbench should, of course, offer an adequate performance and not only for small projects.
4. *Help facility*. A workbench must include adequate 'help' facilities. The developer must be able to ask for help at any time, and the workbench should then provide help information appropriate to the action he is carrying out.
5. *Documentation*. The workbench must have good-quality documentation, which

should preferably be accessible on-line. It is desirable that the workbench includes a tutorial to help the developer when he is first getting acquainted with the product. The installation procedure should be automated to the greatest possible extent.

6. *Continuity of the supplier.* Indicators for this are, for instance, the number of years the supplier has already existed, the supplier's financial position, and the number of copies of the relevant package already sold.

7. *Support for the package.* The supplier must be willing to give a guarantee that serious problems will be solved within a specific time-limit – say 24 hours. There must also be good 'hot-line' support. The supplier must give the developers a say in determining modifications and additions to be made to the package. Courses in the use of the package must be available. Preferably there should be an active users' club.

8. *Price and terms of delivery.* The price is by no means the least important feature of a workbench. There are enormous differences in this respect, which are not always justified by differences in the functional qualities of the respective workbenches. Preferably, there should be a possibility – free or otherwise – to take the package on trial for a while. It must at least be possible to obtain a demonstration version of the package.

9. *Hardware and software requirements.* Points which matter here include: the make and type of computer(s) on which the workbench runs, its internal and external memory requirements, graphics cards that have to be present and data communications facilities needed. Another important factor is the other software which must be present before the workbench can be installed and can run; consider, for example, text editors, DBMSs and data communication software. The cost of a workbench can be significantly increased if specific hardware and/ or software has to be purchased solely for its installation.

10. *Infrastructural considerations.* An analyst workbench or ISEE (and any hardware and software to be purchased in combination with it) must fit into the organization's technical infrastructure. Generally the organization already has one or a number of DBMSs, an (independent) DDS, a fourth-generation development environment, tele-processing monitors, networks, etc.

14.2 TYPES OF ANALYST WORKBENCH

The analyst workbenches that have been released or announced so far differ quite considerably in the degree of their coupling to a specific method or set of methods. On the basis of this criterion, tools can be divided into the following classes:

1. GENERAL-PURPOSE DRAWING TOOLS
Practically any diagram can be drawn using this kind of tool. An example in this category is MacDraw, from Apple. The general-purpose drawing programs are, however, less useful as supporting tools for methods and techniques, since they have no knowledge of the rules for specific diagram types. For example, a particular type

of diagram may have a rule that a flow must always have an object as its source and as its destination, and when an object is deleted from a diagram all incoming and outgoing flows should consequently be deleted. General-purpose drawing aids are not acquainted with rules of this kind. A more serious deficiency of these 'automated pencils' is that, as far as the tool is concerned, a diagram is nothing but an array of pixels (image points) which are set either on or off. No coupling to the data dictionary is possible because the separate objects in the diagram are not recognized as such.

These deficiencies do not, of course, alter the fact that tools of this class can solve a part of the set of problems surrounding the use of structure methods and techniques. Such tools can considerably speed up the drawing and redrawing of diagrams. In combination with a good word processor, they can form a simple, cheap and effective support for the developer.

2. TOOLS SUPPORTING A SPECIFIC METHOD OR METHODOLOGY

By far the largest proportion of the tools currently available are designed to support a specific method/technique or a set of associated methods/techniques. Examples are the IEW of KnowledgeWare, and PROMOD of GEI. For an overview of available analyst workbenches, the reader is referred to various articles on this subject in the trade press (e.g. Hall and Keuffel, 1987; Mair, 1987; Stamps, 1987), reports (e.g. Martin, 1987) and conference proceedings (e.g. DCI, 1987).

As these overviews show, the Yourdon school (dataflow diagrams, structure charts, state transition diagrams) is currently very popular with the suppliers of workbenches. This is because the majority of available workbenches originate from the US, where Yourdon-based methods have a leading position. Among developers of real-time and embedded systems, there is particular interest in the books of Ward and Mellor (1985), and Hatley and Pirbhai (1987), in which the real-time version of the Yourdon method is described.

Some automated tools support more than one method or methodology. The most prominent example of this kind of tool is Excelerator, the first commercially successful package on the CASE market. Among the methods/techniques supported are Structured Analysis, entity-relationship modeling, and Jackson Structured Programming (JSP).

3. CUSTOMIZABLE TOOLS

A study of popular diagramming techniques shows that they do not differ fundamentally from one another. Sometimes it is only the notation that differs: one technique may use an ellipse while another insists on a rectangle. Very often, different representations for the same concepts have been chosen, simply for business reasons.

Because of the similarities among the diagramming techniques, it is possible to create tools that in principle can support any of them. There is a great need for such customizable tools, particularly within large organizations. Because of the non-availability on the market of integrated methodologies that support the entire development process, large organizations have often in the past developed and realized their own methodologies. For this purpose, use has generally been made of methods and techniques developed elsewhere, complemented by internally developed methods; the resulting combination is often unique. In this situation, if the company is not prepared to develop its own workbench, or to change its methodology, it may be necessary to adopt an adaptable package. The same applies to users of less popular and less widespread methods.

Customizable tools must allow their users to define the structure of the data dictionary, to define the *icons* (symbols) which are used in the various diagram types and to specify the design rules which are part of the methodology. A few examples of such adaptable tools are the MAESTRO 'Graphical WorkStation' from Philips/ Softlab, 'ManagerView' from MSP (the supplier of the mainframe DDS DATAMAN- AGER) and the Virtual Software Factory (VSF) of Systematica. Excelerator can be adapted to a preferred method using the product 'XL/Customizer'.

The adaptability of a workbench may also relate to the navigation facility. Some workbenches include a facility for defining what activities must be performed in sequence to arrive at a given (part) product. An example of a tool of this kind is MAESTRO from Softlab/Philips. With this facility, the project model according to, for example, Arthur Andersen's Method/1 could be input.

It must be recognized that implementing an in-house methodology into a customizable workbench can require a large investment of effort. In the first place, it is necessary to do a detailed analysis of the methodology. It will then often become apparent that the methodology is not worked out well enough to enable implementation in the form of an automated tool. In the second place, this implementation will itself demand a fairly large amount of work, particularly if it is required to support the more complex rules. Thirdly, the modified workbench will have to be documented, courses will have to be set up, and the resulting whole will have to be supported and distributed. Finally, it will be necessary to maintain the modified workbench and its documentation. Maintenance will be necessary both for new versions of the standard workbench and the product used for carrying out the modifications, and for new versions of the methodology supported. Additionally, the organization itself will usually have to take responsibility for the development of any conversion programs that may be needed.

However, the investments associated with implementing the in-house methodology on a customizable workbench will sometimes be small in comparison with the investments the organization has already made in developing and introducing that methodology, and in comparison with the investment that would be necessary for migration to a different methodology. In these circumstances, choosing an adaptable workbench is obviously the very best path to follow.

Chapter 15

Fourth-generation Languages

Like all languages, programming languages make possible the transfer of information between a possessor of knowledge and someone (or something) who needs that knowledge. In the case of a programming language, the 'transmitter' of information is the developer of information systems and the 'receiver' is a computer. In the first instance, programming languages were strongly computer oriented. The programmer was obliged to learn the language of the computer to make his intention clear. However, programming languages have undergone a marked evolution during which they have become progressively closer to natural language.

Generally, programming languages are divided into a number of generations. The first-generation programming languages were the 'machine codes'. The programmer issued instructions by entering an (often well-nigh interminable) list of ones and zeros; there was no interpretation or compilation step. Consequently, the programming of computers was a time-consuming and labor-intensive process. The errors that were almost inevitable in a machine-code program were also exceedingly difficult to localize.

Some improvement in this situation came about with the rise in the fifties of the (symbolic) assembler languages. These languages enabled the programmer to use symbolic addresses instead of physical hardware addresses, and to give instructions in the form of mnemonics. Examples of assemblers are SPS, BAL and EASYCODER (Martin, 1985). This second generation of languages is still in use for those applications that have to make very efficient use of hardware (embedded systems, computer games, etc.)

In the sixties, languages of the third generation – the 'high-level' languages – appeared. Well-known examples of such languages are ALGOL, FORTRAN, PL/1, COBOL, Pascal, ADA, BASIC (which became very popular after the arrival of microcomputers) and C (popular in the UNIX environment). In 1969 some 120 programming languages were in existence (Sammet, 1969), most of which have already disappeared. One statement in a third-generation language generally corresponds to a number of instructions in machine code. This is in contrast to assemblers, where a 1:1 ratio generally prevails. Programming in a third-generation language is thus less labour intensive than assembler programming: the compiler or interpreter takes over a great deal of the work.

Fourth-generation languages (or VHLLs, as they are sometimes called) continue this trend, and relieve the application system developer of even more work. The most significant feature of these languages is that they free the developer from much – or even all – concern about the procedural aspects of a program. The first three generations of programming languages oblige the programmer to state what actions the computer must execute, and in what sequence, in order to arrive at the required result. A fourth-generation language, on the other hand, requires the developer to describe the criteria that a solution must satisfy; the compiler or interpreter then determines what actions will lead to the desired result. Fourth-generation languages are thus, to a greater extent than languages of the third generation, 'problem oriented', or 'non-procedural'. The developer can concentrate on the nature of the problem, rather than on the way in which the problem must be solved.

15.1 CHARACTERISTICS OF FOURTH-GENERATION LANGUAGES

In recent years there has been vehement discussion about whether various products that have been labelled as 'fourth generation' do or do not merit that description. The confusion in this area is considerable as there is no generally accepted definition of the term 'fourth-generation language'. Many development tools which should be classed as 'fourth-generation' have been in existence for years. The muddle is further exacerbated by the designation 'language'. In the fourth generation, communication between developer and machine takes place not only by the exchanging of a stream of characters, but also through many different means of expression. 'Programming' takes place partly by the filling in of screens or by giving examples (see, for instance, Query By Example (Martin, 1985)), etc. These means of expression do not fit into the usual interpretation of the term 'programming language'; therefore, people often prefer to speak of fourth-generation *tools* rather than fourth-generation *languages*. However, it must be realized that the term 'language' is none the less correct. Every form of expression used as a means of communication deserves the designation 'language'. Before written language, humans used sign languages, body language and languages of images. In computing, new types of language are being introduced rapidly. The information analyst makes use of diagram techniques to communicate with his colleagues, and end-users communicate with the computer increasingly by means of icons (which quickly became popular after the introduction of the Apple Macintosh). Fourth-generation languages break partly with the traditional form in which the programmer communicates with the computer (a stream of characters), but they are just as much languages as are traditional programming languages such as COBOL.

Whereas in the third generation a clear distinction can be made between the programming language itself and the software that supports it (the compiler), in the fourth generation the language and the language-supporting software are intimately connected. To avoid clouding the discussion, however, it is recommended that a distinction between these two is maintained. Here we use the term 'fourth-generation language' to denote the form of expression that the developer uses for communicating with the computer (equivalent to the third-generation programming language), and for convenience we refer to the software that supports this language as 'fourth-generation software' (equivalent to the compiler in the third generation). When we speak of 'fourth-generation tools' we mean the combination of these two components.

Although, as stated, there is no clear extant definition of 'fourth-generation language', such languages do have a number of features that distinguish them from third-generation languages (Martin, 1985). They are more problem oriented, they are friendlier in use and they are often only suitable for a restricted application area. These characteristics are discussed briefly below.

HIGHER LEVEL OF NON-PROCEDURALITY
As has already been stated, fourth-generation languages have a higher level of non-procedurality than those of the third generation. The developer specifies the result of a process, and does not specify what course that process must take. It is very easy to see whether a language really is fully non-procedural. In a procedural language, the sequence of statements determines the result of a program. In a non-procedural language the developer describes the result of a process and interchanging any pair of statements should have no effect.

Most screen painters, report generators and query processors are driven purely by non-procedural statements. However, a few of the fourth-generation languages such as NOMAD and Natural consist rather of a mixture of procedurality and non-procedurality. For example, these languages allow IF and WHILE constructions in addition to non-procedural statements for retrieving the required data from the database and printing out the results.

The non-procedural character of fourth-generation languages asserts itself most strongly in the conciseness of software written in such languages. Typically, these programs contain far fewer statements than their equivalents in third-generation languages. This is not surprising, seeing that the average program in a third-generation language comprises for some 80 to 90 per cent of instructions aimed at guiding the flow of the program along correct lines and at providing a user-friendly interface. Fourth-generation languages are oriented towards the problem, and make extensive use of defaults. If, for example, the developer makes no stipulations about the layout of a report, the software will choose a suitable layout. The compiler or interpreter makes 'intelligent' assumptions about the user's wishes.

It is often said that use of a fourth-generation language has serious disadvantages for both performance and internal storage requirements of applications. Although the existence of these effects can not be altogether denied, it must be remembered that they are in no way inherent to the non-procedurality of such languages. In fact, the higher level of non-procedurality means that, in principle, more efficient applications can be realized using fourth-generation than using third-generation languages; the compiler 'understands' the application better, giving a possibility for optimization.

However, suppliers of fourth-generation software have in the past concentrated more on expanding the functionality of their products than on taking measures to raise the efficiency of applications realized by use of these. In a growing number of cases efforts are presently being made in respect of improvement of performance (Cobb, 1985). It is therefore quite conceivable that in the near future more efficient applications will be realizable with fourth-generation languages than with such languages as COBOL or Pascal.

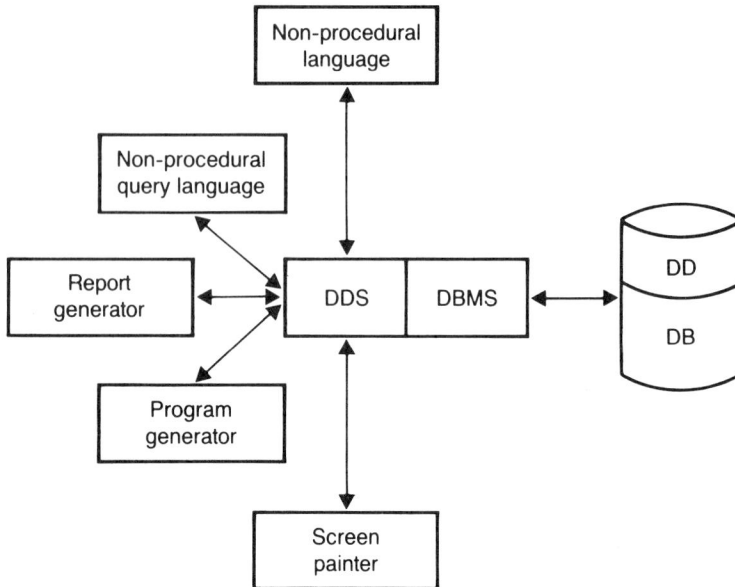

Figure 15.1 An integrated fourth-generation development environment.

FRIENDLIER IN USE

Fourth-generation tools simplify the realization process to a high degree. The software supporting fourth-generation languages is generally many times more user friendly than the equivalent in the third generation: the compiler. In many cases, fourth-generation software 'holds the user's hand' and leads the way step by step through the development process. Additionally, many different interaction mechanisms are available. For example, the developer is presented with menus, and fills in screens or gives the computer examples of the desired result. Often there is a kind of dialogue between the developer and the computer, in which the computer directly draws the user's attention to errors, and immediately asks for clarification in the event of ambiguities. Interpreters are available in most fourth-generation environments, so that the developer does not have to endure a lengthy compilation in order to localize errors in the program. Sometimes the environment also contains a compiler to generate an efficient product as a final development step.

A particularly significant advantage of some fourth-generation tools is the integration of all development facilities into a single environment (see Fig. 15.1). Some prominent suppliers in this respect are Cullinet, Software AG, CINCOM and Mathematica. In fourth-generation development environments of this kind, the following components are generally present:

1. An active, integrated DDS.
2. A relational or semi-relational DBMS (one with a relational shell).
3. A non-procedural language for maintaining the database.
4. A non-procedural query language.

5. A non-procedural language for report generation.
6. A powerful procedural language or program generator.
7. A screen painter.

The developer can obtain free access to the data dictionary, generate screens and reports, and write and test programs without having to leave the environment. Additionally, the fourth-generation environment protects the developer from such things as TP-monitors and job control language (JCL). In consequence, it is much simpler to learn 'programming' in a fourth-generation environment than in a traditional third-generation language. Thus, relatively inexperienced automation staff can quickly be deployed to productive effect.

LIMITED AREA OF APPLICABILITY PER LANGUAGE
The hundred-plus fourth-generation languages currently available, and their associated software, show large differences in power and capabilities. With some fourth-generation tools it is possible to build a transaction-processing system that gives a good performance even under a heavy load; other tools, in comparison, soon fail when the system load becomes too high or the database too large, and are therefore more suitable for decision support systems. Some languages can be used only in specific application areas; some are very well suited to end-user development of simple applications, while others are specifically intended for professional system developers. It is much more important for fourth- than for third-generation languages for the choice of language to be carefully matched to the problem to be solved.

   Because of the relatively short period that fourth-generation languages have been in existence, there are (apart from the query language SQL) no standards in this field. There is simply not enough known about the requirements of the dialogue between developer and development software, the syntactic constructions that must be available, etc. Which of the integrated fourth-generation development environments and their associated languages will ultimately survive can still only be conjectured.

HIGHER PRODUCTIVITY
The higher level of non-procedurality and greater user friendliness of fourth-generation tools results in applications being realized many times more quickly in a fourth-generation than in a third-generation language. In Chapter 2, reference was made to a study by Rudolph (1983), from which it appeared that applications can be realized (according to the complexity of the application) 20 to 50 times more quickly using the fourth-generation language LINC than using COBOL. Some other fourth-generation languages also lead to an acceleration of a similar order of magnitude in the realization phase.

15.2 TYPES OF FOURTH-GENERATION LANGUAGE

Fourth-generation languages can be broadly classified along two dimensions: the *complexity of the applications* that they can be used to develop (from simple applications

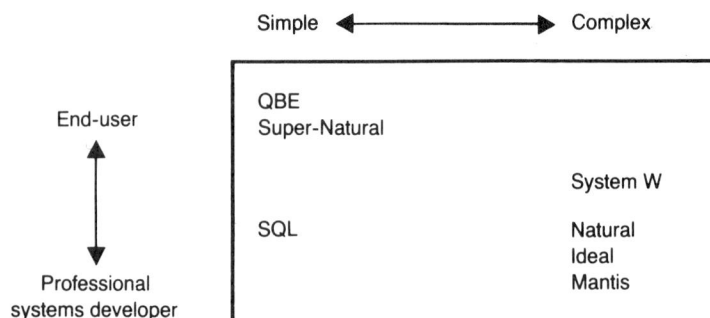

Figure 15.2 Various types of fourth-generation language.

for producing straightforward reports on database contents to fairly complex applications in which the data is subjected to extensive processing), and the *user category* for which the tool is suitable (from end-users without any knowledge of automation to professional systems developers). This is shown in Fig. 15.2 in which, for the purposes of illustration, the position of some existing fourth-generation languages is also indicated. The remainder of this section discusses these two dimensions in more detail.

COMPLEXITY OF THE APPLICATION

The complexity of an application can be expressed in terms of (1) the complexity of the (retrieval) operations performed on the database and (2) the complexity of the processing that the data has to undergo. The simplest applications consist of making a selection from a single table (with a simple selection criterion) and printing a report, without any processing of the selected data. The complexity of an application becomes greater as the selection criteria become more complex, and the selected data have to undergo increasingly complicated processing.

As long as an application is primarily aimed at the selection of data from a database, and the data have to undergo little or no processing, the developer can make use of *non-procedural query languages* or *report generation languages*. These languages differ in the complexity of the queries that can be formulated. Sometimes queries may refer only to records of one specific type; with more advanced languages, queries can also be formulated about records of different types which satisfy complex selection criteria. Some examples of non-procedural query languages are Query By Example (QBE) and SQL from IBM, Mathematica's RAMIS Query and RAMIS ENGLISH (a natural language interface to RAMIS Query), and OnLine Query from Cullinet.

As soon as there is any question of data being processed, the purely non-procedural languages can no longer be used, and the developer has to turn to those fourth-generation languages that also allow procedural statements. To distinguish these languages from the non-procedural query languages they are often referred to by the term *fourth-generation programming languages*. These languages can do anything that COBOL can, but also provide the developer with more powerful tools and statements. Examples of languages belonging to this category are Ideal from Applied Data Research, Natural from Software AG, and Mantis from CINCOM.

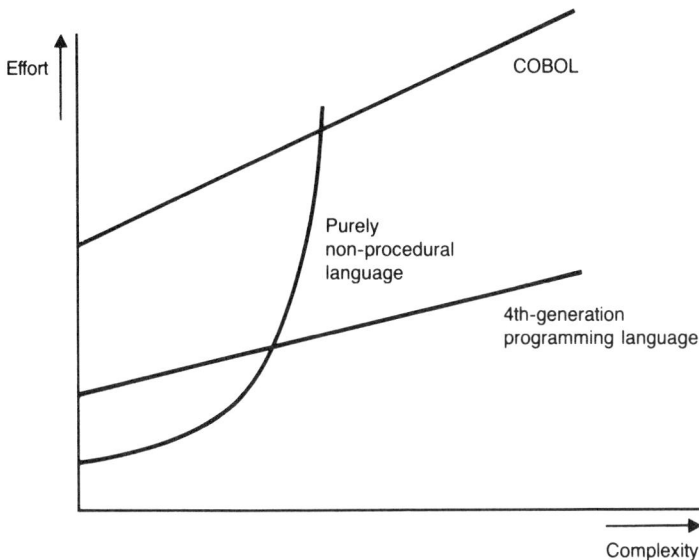

Figure 15.3 Complexity of the application and type of fourth-generation language. (*Source*: Adapted from Martin (1985). Reprinted with permission.)

Obviously, very simple applications can also be realized with languages of this kind. In general, however, for simple applications a purely non-procedural language is preferable to a language that has a mixture of procedural and non-procedural statements, because of the complexity of languages in the latter category. This is shown in Fig. 15.3. This figure also indicates, for comparison, the amount of effort required to realize an application in a third-generation language.

In some applications, data has to undergo complex or specific processing. Consider, for example, decision-support systems in which statistical processing is frequently used. The typical fourth-generation language usually falls short of the mark here. To realize such applications, a tailor-made language has to be used. Languages of this kind are sometimes referred to as *specialist fourth generation languages*. Among languages specifically suited to building decision-support systems are Express, IFPS and System W. Another example of a specialist fourth-generation language is MIMS, a language specifically suited to the building of logistics applications.

USER CATEGORY

With the arrival of fourth-generation languages, programming computers is no longer exclusively the territory of the systems professional. Many of the fourth-generation languages already show some similarity to natural language. Additionally, fourth-generation software often leads the developer through the development process. Developing applications thereby comes within the scope of end-users. The extent to which end-users will be able to use a fourth-generation language will depend on two factors: their ability or skill in the area of information system development, and the user friendliness of the available language.

Increasing numbers of end-users have a substantial knowledge of automation. Sometimes the only thing that distinguishes them from systems professionals is that they are developing an information system for their own use, and not for others. In contrast to these 'semi-professionals', however, a typical organization still also houses a number of users who lack any knowledge of – or affinity towards – automation. The majority of users in an organization usually fall somewhere between these two extremes.

Fourth-generation languages display large differences in the respect of user friendliness. Some query languages almost enable the user to formulate queries in the natural language, any ambiguities in the formulation of the query being resolved interactively. An example of such a query language is RAMIS ENGLISH, from Mathematica. A query language such as Query By Example, however, uses a completely different interaction mechanism, in which the user enters selection criteria in tables that represent the structure of the database. Yet other languages make an extensive use of menus (for example, Super-Natural from Software AG). SQL, on the other hand, gives hardly any support to the user in formulating a question.

The typical user can generally get by using user-friendly query languages. As soon as the nature of the query becomes more complex, however, less user-friendly query languages such as SQL quickly become unsuited to the average end-user. Such fourth-generation programming languages as Ideal and Natural are more complex in character than the query language, and not every user will be able to use them. The specialist languages are also often fairly complex, often being aimed at specialists in a particular field who after a short period are generally capable of making effective use of such a language.

Before end-users are allowed to develop applications themselves, however, certain precautions must be taken. Some languages make it possible for the user to modify the contents of a database, and in these cases it must be ensured that the end-user can change only that data for which he is authorized. It is also necessary to forestall situations where end-users start building systems which expand to become the mainstay of their department, but are neither documented nor maintainable. Finally, it must be reasonably ascertained whether the users concerned really are able to handle the given facilities correctly. In the case of the rather more complex query languages, for example, there is a danger that the user may choose a way of formulating a query that seems correct at first sight, but in fact contains faults that are only likely to be revealed on closer examination. The user will then take decisions – perhaps important ones – on the basis of output that looks acceptable in all respects, but in fact answers a different question from that intended.

Chapter 16
CASE: The State of the Art

Considering all the problems confronting the typical information systems department nowadays, CASE has become a bitter necessity. Fourth-generation tools and analyst workbenches are in the limelight. CASE tools can already take over a substantial number of tasks from the developer and considerably raise the efficiency and the effectiveness of the development process. However, the present generation of tools still suffers from a number of defects.

This chapter provides some comments about the state of the art in the CASE area at the time of writing. The reader must bear in mind that, in view of the very rapid developments in this field, some of the information in this chapter may have become inaccurate by time of reading.

DATA DICTIONARIES AND EDITORS

Practically all the current products acknowledge that the data dictionary should play a central role within the workbench. It is thus generally possible to store the meta-data that have to be produced in accordance with the methodology. However, there are hardly any workbenches that offer adequate facilities for version control. When the developer wishes to preserve various versions of (sets of) development data, he must make copies himself. The typical workbench does not at present possess a status management facility; the developer must keep his own record of which development data are provisional, which (sets of) development data have already been analyzed and approved, which development data may no longer be modified except in response to a formal change request and so on.

As far as the graphics facilities of the various packages are concerned, there are really no fundamental differences. It may be observed that any lead which a particular workbench may have in this respect is often of a very temporary character. New releases of the various packages follow one another rapidly; today's leader is tomorrow's straggler. Although of course important, the graphics facilities are thus about the last criterion on which one should appraise and select a package.

The majority of the workbenches do not store diagrams but generate them, when required, on the basis of the current contents of the data dictionary. In the workbenches which store not only the contents of diagrams but also the diagrams themselves, problems sometimes arise when the development data are used by more than one person and are, for that reason, frequently transferred from dictionary to dictionary.

The user must then take his own measures to prevent inconsistencies between diagrams and the contents of the data dictionary.

ANALYSIS FACILITIES

One of the areas in which the existing workbenches display big differences is their philosophy concerning prevention of inconsistency and insufficiency in the data dictionary. Some tools try to identify immediately any infringement of the analysis and design rules, and to get the user to correct them straight away. When using a tool that follows this philosophy, the user is repeatedly rapped over the knuckles. Other workbenches, in contrast, tolerate inconsistencies and provide the user with facilities to check at any desired moment whether the results of all the work satisfy the rules embodied in the methods concerned.

Both approaches have advantages and disadvantages. Workbenches of the first type can be used only when the requirements definition has already substantially crystallized; they demand completeness and accuracy at a time when the developer is still searching for answers, and are thus certainly not usable during prototyping. The latter type of workbench leaves the developer more freedom, but he must be disciplined enough to remove the inconsistencies and insufficiencies from the dictionary at the appropriate time.

Various workbenches with an 'open' architecture show considerable differences in the extent to and the ease with which the developer can implement user-specific design rules. For this, some workbenches include a purpose-designed programming language; others offer a number of routines giving access to the workbench dictionary, making it possible to develop programs that check the consistency and completeness of the stored data in a standard programming language such as C or Pascal. A very limited number of workbenches provide a facility to define which user actions should cause a checking routine to be invoked. In the majority of cases, checking routines cannot be activated automatically but must be invoked explicitly by the user of the workbench.

USER-INTERFACE DESIGN AND PROTOTYPING

A growing number of workbenches are equipped with facilities for designing screens and reports. Some workbenches even link the diagrams modeling the flow of data among activities (such as dataflow diagrams) with screens and reports. In such workbenches, screens and reports 'implement' data flows. When designing a screen, the developer links it to a data flow. The workbench then produces a list of the data elements comprising the data flow concerned. Using the mouse, the developer picks up the data elements one by one and puts them down at the desired place. The screens/reports then remain linked to the data flow, so that any changes to the dataflow diagram are immediately reflected in the user interface, and vice versa.

The facilities for designing the dialogue between the end-user and the information system are still fairly limited in the majority of workbenches. In general it is not possible to model which user actions are allowed in the various states the system can be in, and the reaction of the system to the various user actions. The few workbenches that do offer facilities of this type allow the developer to model the dialogue by means of either diagrams or fill-in screens.

The prototyping facilities of most current workbenches are quite limited. After the user interface has been designed, it is in principle possible to generate a prototype showing the user the 'outside' of the system. There are some packages available that offer support here, but there is none as yet available that allows the developer to produce functional prototypes (prototypes that not only model the user interface, but also provide the user with facilities for storing and modifying data, and performing calculations on the stored data). As stated in Section 14.1.4, for that purpose the workbench should comprise, besides a screen painter, report generator and dialogue handler, both a DBMS and a fouth-generation language, or should be very closely coupled to an environment that contains these facilities.

SHARED USE OF META-DATA

The manufacturers of analyst workbenches have so far paid relatively little attention to the way in which analysis and design information can be shared among groups of developers. The majority of products presently available have a stand-alone character, and come complete with their own data dictionary. Although the transfer of meta-data from one dictionary to another is technically not difficult, facilities for exporting and importing meta-data are often not provided. When such facilities are available, all kinds of problems arise when the (sometimes inconsistent) data originating from the various local dictionaries must be integrated into the central data dictionary. It is not yet clear how to ensure that the data in the various local dictionaries can be kept up to date, so that developers can always rely on their 'own' data dictionary giving a reliable image of the state of affairs in the part of the project of interest to them.

INTERFACES WITH OTHER TOOLS

The objective of many of the current CASE suppliers is to provide users with an integrated set of tools that supports all activities taking place in and around the project. This objective has not yet been achieved. Current CASE products support or automate only part of the development process. If analyst workbenches are combined with other tools in an attempt to construct a set of tools to deal with all project activities, it usually becomes apparent that there are overlaps or gaps, that the various products cannot (or not easily) communicate with one another or that they continually confront the developer with a different user interface.

Now that the earlier analyst workbenches are maturing, it is noticeable that their suppliers are beginning to devote more attention to supporting facilities for other project activities. In the great majority of cases, the workbench suppliers do not create these tools themselves but find an add-on product and construct a link with it. The advantage of this strategy is that a powerful addition to the analyst workbench becomes available immediately. The disadvantage is that yet again there are sometimes overlaps or mis-match problems.

An increasing number of workbenches are coupled with facilities for generating (parts of) programs. Usually it is a matter of coupling the workbench to a program generator that is already available in the market. In isolated cases the generator is developed by the suppliers of the workbench themselves. However, with the current tools only very simple applications can be generated completely. Sometimes the generation process is restricted to the conversion of screens and reports designed on the workbench into a format demanded by the target environment (for example MFS running under IMS DB/DC). For complex applications only the program structure can usually be generated; the user has to complete this by providing the program code. A small number of workbenches include facilities for generating a database structure in the DDLs of, for example, ADABAS, IDMS, or Ingres. They do not generate an optimal structure, but rather a 'first cut' that the user can take as a basis for the physical database design.

ANALYST WORKBENCHES AND FOURTH-GENERATION LANGUAGES

A problem area that will demand much attention in the coming years is the connection between analyst workbenches and fourth-generation development environments. Such an environment supports the developer in rapid construction and modification of an application. Strictly, it should not be permitted to modify programs before the application's requirements definition and technical design have been corrected. An increasing number of workbenches are also coupled with program generators. Such a combination makes it possible to generate an information system on the basis of a requirements definition. In the future, maintenance will be done on the requirements definition level, and not on the program level. A direct consequence of this is that there will no longer be any need for a great many of the functions offered to the developer by a fourth-generation development environment.

The suppliers of fourth-generation development aids are extending their products by adding PC-based tools for the earlier phases of the development process. To prevent inconsistencies occurring between the contents of the workbench dictionary on the PC and the dictionary in the fourth-generation environment on the mainframe, items that have already been specified in the workbench dictionary will have to be

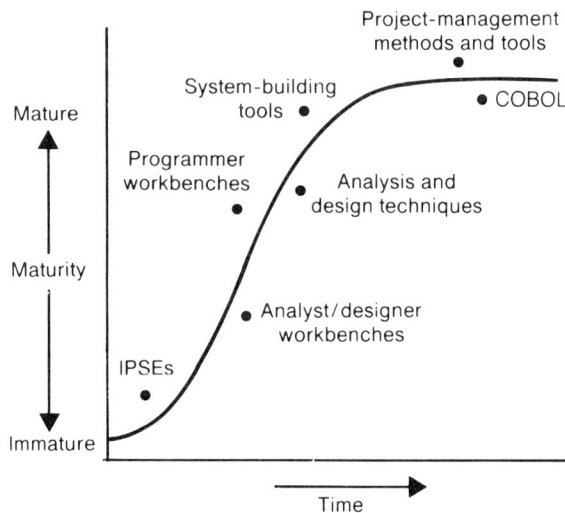

Figure 16.1 Maturity of CASE technology. (*Source*: Butler-Cox Foundation (1987). Reprinted by permission of Butler-Cox & Partners Limited.)

unalterable in the fourth-generation environment. The only way in which a program or database structure can then be modified is through the workbench. This means that part of the functional capabilities offered to the developer by a fourth-generation development environment will have to be transferred to the workbench.

STRATEGY IN THE CASE AREA

It will by now have become clear to the reader that CASE is still in a very early stage of development. This is illustrated in Fig. 16.1. A genuinely integrated set of tools for the entire development process is still some way off. A critical examination of the tools available in the market-place at the moment indicates that the brochures of the workbench suppliers give a rather optimistic view of the actual state of affairs. Very many analyst workbenches are still in a prototype state, or have only recently been released. Thus they have certainly not yet proved themselves in practice.

On the other hand, it is beyond dispute that ISEEs will drastically change the way in which information systems are developed. The restrictions of the various tools will quite certainly be lifted. In addition, in spite of all their shortcomings, the use of these tools can already lead to considerable savings. In most cases, the acquisition of CASE tools can already be justified on the grounds of efficiency improvements alone and the associated direct savings. These tools have the potential to increase the effectiveness of the development process dramatically. CASE technology makes new approaches to system development in general, and requirements definition in particular, both economically and technically feasible. CASE without prototyping is often ineffective; prototyping without CASE is virtually impossible.

Appendix
The ISO Three-level Approach

The aim of exchanging information between a provider and a user of information (also known as a '*transmitter*' and a '*receiver*' respectively) is the passing on of knowledge possessed by the transmitter about certain things, facts or events, in which the receiver is interested. To perform this exchange, they sometimes need the help of an information system which enables them to bridge a distance (the communication function of the information system), and which makes it possible to receive this information at a different point in time from when it was sent (the memory function of the information system).

In order to make the exchange of information possible, it must be cast in a concrete, communicable form. An effective information exchange further requires that both the transmitter and the receiver interpret the representation in the same way. The term '*data*' refers to the concrete *form* in which information is expressed (the symbols and syntax used); the term '*information*' relates to the *meaning* or interpretation of data (the semantics). When an information system is being developed, the developer must attend to both the meaning and the form of information. Another relevant aspect is the way in which data is stored – often termed the '*internal format*'.

In the context of information systems, this distinction between the meaning of information, its various forms of expression and its handling within the computer is known as the 'three-level approach'.[1] At each of the three levels distinguished in this approach, the emphasis is on a different aspect of the information system:

1. The information or conceptual level.
2. The data or external level.
3. The internal or technical level.

At the conceptual level, those matters about which the information system has to provide information (called, in ISO terms, the '*universe of discourse*', often abbreviated to UoD) are modeled. A completely abstract standpoint is taken at this level with respect to the possible forms of external and internal representation. The chief concerns are to examine the structure of that part of the world which is of interest and which must later be depicted in computer applications and databases, and to establish what rules govern its behavior.

At the external level, attention is focused on how the system will manifest itself to its users. At this level, the developer is concerned with the (user-dependent) form of the information. The requirements at the external level will often vary according to the user group. For example, for pragmatic or often merely historical reasons, a given product may be identified by different codes in the commercial and the technical environments in an organization.

At the internal level, attention is paid to all the implementation-dependent aspects. The users of the information system are generally not interested in such aspects, in contrast to the builders of the information system whose primary interest is directed specifically towards the internal level. Matters of concern at this level are, for instance, how the information is represented on various storage media, the efficiency and speed with which these data can be accessed (i.e. made available to the application which asks for them) and how simultaneous use of the data can be controlled.

The three-level principle has been consistently developed in ISO circles into an architecture for information systems, which will undoubtedly have a considerable influence on future developments in the area of DDSs and DSMSs. However, in the context of this book it is the ISO frame of reference that is of interest. Readers who are interested in the consequences of the three-level approach with respect to the architecture of information systems should refer to the relevant ISO report (Griethuysen, 1987). The ISO three-level architecture agrees approximately with the well-known ANSI/SPARC architecture of database systems. A concise description of this architecture can be found in Date (1982), for instance.

BENEFITS OF THE THREE-LEVEL APPROACH

In the past, when data-processing systems were being created the emphasis was placed primarily on the external and internal aspects. Even today, there are numerous methods for information analysis which make no distinction between the actual information need of the user and the representational form in which he wishes to receive the information produced by the system. As the reader will probably be aware, development strategies which are known as 'data-driven' are based on the assumption that data structures are more stable in character than the processes which consume the modelled data. In this perception, during the development of an information system it is first necessary to concentrate on discovering what data is needed, and the relationships among those data.

The three-level approach takes a similar standpoint, but with the extra rider that during information analysis the main emphasis should be placed on the conceptual aspects. Consideration of the way in which the information is to be represented impedes the understanding of the basic information requirements. At the conceptual level things are modelled 'as they really are'. Intuitively, it is quite clear that such an 'essential' model is more stable than one which reflects how particular individuals wish to view that reality.

This outlook is becoming more and more widely accepted. In the development of information systems, attention must first be directed towards deepening insight into that portion of the world about which the system must exchange information, and towards modelling that world at the conceptual level. Only later will the form in which the exchange of information takes place become important, together with the way in which the information system must be internally constructed in order to make such exchange possible. There are an increasing number of methods available to the information analyst for modelling that part of the world in which he is interested, independently of internal and external aspects. Examples of such methods are INFOMOD (a method developed by Philips in the Netherlands (Jardine and Griethuysen, 1987a)) and NIAM (developed in Control Data's Research Laboratory in Brussels (Wintraecken, 1985). These methods are enjoying growing popularity, especially in Europe.

It will be clear from the above that the three-level approach, and especially the emphasis this approach places on the conceptual aspects, leads to a more solid basis for information system development. The three-level approach enables developers to concentrate on those aspects which need attention at a particular moment, and to distance themselves from aspects which are unimportant at that time. In the first phase of the analysis the information analyst will wish to work at a purely conceptual level so that his view of the information problem will not be clouded by various irrelevant considerations concerning the form the system must eventually take. Later in the requirements definition phase, attention will be paid to the users' requirements and wishes regarding the way in which the system presents itself. Neither the information analyst nor the users have to concern themselves deeply about the way in which the system will later be realized; although naturally it is important not to lose sight of the technical aspects completely.

NOTE

1. The term 'level' can be rather misleading because it gives the (inaccurate) impression that there is a hierarchical relationship between the three aspects. This is not the case, and was in no way so intended by the ISO. Unfortunately 'level' has already become established. It might have been better had a term such as 'realm' or 'aspect' been adopted.

References and Further Reading

REFERENCES

Ahituv, N., Hadass, M. and Neumann, S. (1984) 'A flexible approach to information system development', *MIS Quarterly*, June, 69–78.

Alavi, M. (1984a) 'An assessment of the prototyping approach to information systems development', *Communications of the ACM*, **27** (6), June, 556–63.

Alavi, M. (1984b) 'The evolution of information systems development approach: some field observations', *Data Base*, Spring, 19–24.

Albrecht, A. J. (1979) 'Measuring application development productivity', in: *Proceedings IBM Development Symposium*, Monterey, CA, October 14–17.

Alloway, R. M. and Quillard, J. A. (1983) 'User managers systems needs', *MIS Quarterly*, **7** (2), 27–42.

Baber, R. L. (1982) *Software Reflected: The Socially Responsible Programming of Our Computers*, North-Holland Publishing Company, Amsterdam/New York/Oxford.

Bell, T. E., Bixler, D. C. and Dyer, M. E. (1977) 'An extendable approach to computer-aided software requirements engineering', in: *IEEE Transactions on Software Engineering*, **SE–3** (1) January, 49–59.

Berrisford, T. and Wetherbe, J. (1979) 'Heuristic development: a redesign of systems design', *MIS Quarterly*, March, 11–19.

Boar, B. H. (1984) *Application Prototyping: A Requirements Definition Strategy for the 80s*, John Wiley & Sons Inc., New York.

Boehm, B. W. (1981) *Software Engineering Economics*, Prentice Hall, Englewood Cliffs, NJ.

Boehm, B. W., Gray, T. E. and Seewaldt, T. (1984) 'Prototyping versus specifying: a multiproject experiment', *IEEE Transactions on Software Engineering*, **SE–10** (3), May, 290–302.

Butler-Cox Foundation (1987) *Using System Development Methods*, Research Report 57, June.

Cerveny, R. P., Garrity, E. J. and Sanders, G. L. (1986) 'The application of prototyping to systems development: a rationale and model', *Journal of management information systems*, Fall, **III** (2), 53–62.

Chen, P. P. (ed.) (1983) *Entity-relationship Approach to Information Modelling and Analysis*, North-Holland, Amsterdam.

Cobb, R. H. (1985) 'In praise of 4GLs', *Datamation*, July 15, 90–6

Codd, E. F. (1970) 'A relational model of data for large shared data banks', *Communications of the ACM*, June, **13** (6), 377–87.

Commission of the European Communities, (1986) *Esprit: the First Phase Progress and Results*, COM(86) 687 Final, Brussels, 8 Dec.

Cutts, G. (1987) *Structured Analysis and Design Methodology*, Paradigm Publishing, London.

Date, C. J. (1982) *An Introduction to Database Systems: Volume 1*, Third Edition, The Systems Programming Series, Addison-Wesley, Reading, MA.

Davis, G. B. (1982) 'Strategies for information requirements determination', *IBM Systems Journal*, **21** (1), 4–30.

DCI (1987) *Proceedings CASE Symposium*, Digital Consulting Inc., Andover, MA.

Dearnley, P. A. and Mayhew, P. J. (1983) 'In favour of system prototypes and their integration into the systems development cycle', *The Computer Journal*, **26** (1), 36–42.

DeMarco, T. (1978) *Structured Analysis and System Specification*, Prentice Hall, Englewood Cliffs, NJ.

Diebold Group (1982) *The Diebold Information Technology Scan*, Document Number 209T, The Diebold Group, New York.

Diebold Group (1983) *New Guidelines for Application Packages*, Document Number 221S, July, The Diebold Group, New York.

Earl, M. J. (1982) 'Prototype systems for accounting, information and control', *Data Base*, Winter-Spring, 39–46.

EDP Analyzer (1984) 'Using fourth generation languages and prototyping', *EDP Analyzer*, Special Report, Canning Publications, Vista, CA.

EDP Analyzer (1985) 'Speeding up application development', *EDP Analyzer*, Canning Publications, Vista, CA.

Fagan, M. E. (1976) 'Design and code inspections to reduce errors in program development', *IBM Systems Journal*, **15** (3), 182–211.

Flint, D., Moreton, R. and Woodward, C. (1983) *Cost-Effective Systems Development and Maintenance*, Report Series No. 36, August, The Butler-Cox Foundation, London.

Floyd, C. (1984) 'A systematic look at prototyping', in: Budde, R., Kuhlenkamp, K., Mathiassen, L., and Züllighoven, H. (eds), *Approaches to Prototyping*, pp. 1–19, Springer-Verlag, Berlin.

Galbraith, J. (1973) *Designing Complex Organizations*, Addison-Wesley, Reading, MA.

Galbraith, J. R. (1977) *Organization Design*, Addison-Wesley, Reading, MA.

Gane, C. P. and Sarson, T. (1979) *Structured Systems Analysis*, Prentice Hall, Englewood Cliffs, NJ.

Gremillion, L. L. and Pyburn, P. (1983) 'Breaking the systems bottleneck', *Harvard Business Review*, March–April, 130–7.

Griethuysen, J. J. van (ed.) (1987) *Concepts and Terminology for the Conceptual Schema and the Information Base*, ISO Report ISO TC97–TR 9007, ISO, Geneva.

Guimaraes, T. (1987) 'Prototyping: orchestrating for success', *Datamation*, Dec. 1, 101–6.

Hall, D. and Keuffel, W. (1987) 'System design from the ground up', *Computer Language*, January, 105–21.

Hatley, D. J. and Pirbhai, I. A. (1987) *Strategies for Real-time System Specification*, Dorset House, New York.

Hausen, H. L. and Mullerburg, M. (1982) 'Software engineering environments: state of the art, problems, and perspectives', in: *Proceedings IEEE Compsac 82*, pp. 326–35, IEEE Computer Society Press, Silver Spring.

Hice, G. F., Turner, I. and Cashwell, L. F. (1987) *SDM–System Development Methodology*, Elsevier, Amsterdam.

Hirschheim, R. A. (1983) 'Assessing participative systems design: some conclusions from an exploratory study', *Information and Management*, No. 6, 317–27.

Horowitz, E., Kemper, A. and Narasimhan, B. (1985) 'A survey of application generators', *IEEE Software*, Jan., 40–54, Long Beach, CA.

Hruschka, P. (1983) 'The software engineering environment PROMOD', in: *Proceedings ESA/ESTEC Software Engineering Seminar*, October, pp. 59–63, Noordwijk.

Iivari, J. (1984) 'Prototyping in the context of information systems design', in: Budde *et al.* (eds), *Approaches to Prototyping*, pp. 261–77, Springer-Verlag, Berlin.

Jardine, D. A. and Griethuysen, J. J. van (1987a) 'A logic-based information modelling language', *Data and Knowledge Engineering*, **2**, 59–81.

Jardine, D. A. and Griethuysen, J. J. van (1987b) 'Specification of information systems operations in INFOMOD', *Data and Knowledge Engineering*, **2** 177–90.

Jones, C. (1986) *Programming Productivity*, McGraw-Hill, New York.

Kauber, P. G. (1985) 'Prototyping: not a method but a philosophy', *Journal of Systems Management*, September, 28–33.

Kent, W. (1983) 'A simple guide to five normal forms in relational database theory', *Communications of the ACM*, **26** (2), February, 120–5.

Kull, D. (1985) 'Tooling up for design', *Computer Decisions*, **17** (3), February 12, 38–48, 142.

Land, F. (1982) 'Adapting to changing user requirements', *Information and Management*, No. 5, 59–75:

Längle, G. B., Leitheiser, R. L. and Naumann, J. D. (1984) ' A survey of applications systems prototyping in industry', *Information and Management*, **7**, 273–84.

Law, D. (1985) *Prototyping: A State of the Art Report*, NCC, Manchester.

Lientz, B., Swanson, E. and Tompkins, G. (1978) 'Characteristics of application software maintenance', *Communications of the ACM*, **21** (6) (June), 466–71.

Lissandre, M., Lagier, P., Skalli, A. and Massié, H., (1984) *Specif – A Specification Assistance System*, Institut de Génie Logiciel (IGL), Paris.

Lundeberg, M., Goldkuhl, G. and Nilsson, A. (1981) *Information Systems Development. A Systematic Approach*, Prentice Hall, Englewood Cliffs, NJ.

Lyons, T. G. L. (1986) 'The public tool interface in software engineering environments', *Software Engineering Journal* (special issue on software tools in industry), November, 254–9.

Mair, P. (1986) *Integrated Project Support Environments: State of the Art Report*, The National Computing Centre Ltd, Oxford Road, Manchester M1 7ED, England.

Mair, P. (1987) 'Integrated project support environments', *Electronics and Power*, May.

Mann, R. I. and Watson, H. J. (1984) 'A contingency model for user involvement in DSS development', *MIS Quarterly*, March, 27–38.

Marca, D.A. and McGowan, C. L. (1988) *SADT: Structured Analysis and Design Technique*, McGraw-Hill, New York.

Martin, J. (1982a) *Application Development without Programmers*, Prentice Hall, Englewood Cliffs, NJ.

Martin, J. (1982b) *Strategic Data Planning Methodologies*, Prentice Hall, London.

Martin, J. (1985) *Fourth Generation Languages, Volume 1: Principles*, Prentice Hall, Englewood Cliffs, NJ.

Martin, J. (ed.) (1987) *Computer-Aided Software Engineering*, The James Martin Productivity Series Volume 6, Savant Institute, Carnforth, Lancs.

Mayhew, P. J. and Dearnly, P. A. (1987) 'An alternative prototyping classification', *The Computer Journal*, **30** (6), 481–4.

McFarlan, F. W. and McKenney, J. L. (1983) *Corporate Information Systems Management: The Issues Facing Senior Executives*, Richard D. Irwin, Illinois.

Naumann, J. D., Davis, G. B. and McKeen, J. D. (1980) 'Determining information requirements: a contingency method for selection of a requirements assurance strategy', *The Journal of Systems and Software*, No. 1, 273–81.

Naumann, J D. and Jenkins, A. M. (1982) 'Prototyping: the new paradigm for systems development', *MIS Quarterly*, September, 29–44.

Page-Jones, M. (1980) *The Practical Guide to Structured Systems Design*, Yourdon Press, New York.

Podolsky, J. L. (1977) 'Horace builds a cycle', *Datamation*, November, 162–8.

Riddle, W, E. (1984) 'Advancing the state of the art in software system prototyping', in: Budde, R., Kuhlenkamp, K., Mathlassen, L. and Züllighoven, H. (eds), *Approaches to Prototyping*, pp. 19–27, Springer-Verlag, Berlin.

Rosenberger, R. B. (1981) 'The information center', *Proceedings SHARE No. 56*, Session M372, March.

Rudolph, E. E. (1983) *Productivity in Computer Application Development*, Department of Management Studies Working Paper No. 9, March, University of Auckland.

Sammet, J. E. (1969) *Programming Languages*, Prentice Hall Inc., Englewood Cliffs, NJ.

Santos, B. L. Dos (1986) 'A management approach to systems development projects', *Journal of Systems Management*, August, 35–41.

Schein, E. H. (1969) *Process Consultation: its Role in Organization Development*, Addison-Wesley, Reading, MA.

Schonberger, R. J. (1980) 'MIS design: a contingency approach', *MIS Quarterly*, March, 13–20.

Shneiderman, B. (1980) *Software Psychology: Human Factors in Computer and Information Systems*, Winthrop Publishers Inc., Cambridge, MA.

Shomenta, J., Kamp, G., Hanson, B. and Simpson, B. (1983) 'The application approach worksheet: an evaluative tool for matching new development methods with appropriate applications', *MIS Quarterly*, December, 1–10.

Smith, S. L. (1986) 'Standards versus guidelines for designing user interface software', *Behaviour and Information Technology*, **5** (1), 47–61.

Smith, G. L., Stephens, S. A., Tripp, L. L. and Warren, W. L. (1980) 'Incorporating usability into requirements engineering tools', *Proceedings ACM 80*, Nashville.

Stamps, D. (1987) 'CASE: cranking out productivity', *Datamation*, July 1, 48–58.

Teichroew, D. and Hershey, E. A. (1977) 'PSL/PSA: a computer-aided technique for structured documentation and analysis of information processing system', *IEEE Transactions on Software Engineering*, **SE-3** (1), January, 41–58.

Umeh, F. N. (1985) 'Automated design tool can pay back in easily modified, fully documented systems', *Small Systems World*, No. 5, May.

Ward, P. T. and Mellor, S. J. (1985) *Structured Development for Real-time Systems*, Preliminary edition, Volumes 1, 2 and 3, Yourdon Press Computing Series, Prentice Hall, Englewood Cliffs, NJ.

Wetherbe, J. C. and Leitheiser, R. L. (1985) 'Information centers: a survey of services, decisions, problems, and successes', *Journal of Information Systems Management*, Summer, 3–10.

Wintraecken, J. J. V. R., (1985) *Informatie-analyse Volgens NIAM in Theorie en Praktijk*, Academic Service, Den Haag.

Xephon, (1983) *Reducing the Applications Backlog*, Xephon Consultancy Report.

Yourdon, E. (1986) 'What ever happened to structured analysis?', *Datamation*, June 1, 133–8.

Yourdon, E. and Constantine, L. L. (1979) *Structured Design*, Prentice Hall, Englewood Cliffs, NJ.

Zelkowitz, M. V., Show, A. C. and Gannon, J. D. (1979) *Principles of Software Engineering and Design*, Prentice Hall, Englewood Cliffs, NJ.

FURTHER READING

Prototyping

Andrews, W. C. (1983) 'Prototyping information systems', *Journal of Systems Management*, September, 16–18.

Appleton, D. S. (1983) 'Data-driven prototyping', *Datamation*, November, 259–68.

Beregi, W. G. (1984) 'Architecture prototyping in the software engineering environment', *IBM Systems Journal*, **23** (1), 4–18.

Blum, B. I. (1982) 'The life cycle – a debate over alternate models', *ACM Sigsoft Engineering Notes*, **7** (4), October, 18–20.

Blum, B. I. (1983) 'Still more about rapid prototyping', *ACM Sigsoft Software Engineering Notes*, **8** (3), July, 9–11.

Boar, B. H. (1983) 'Prototyping: giving users a working model for applications development', *Computerworld*, September 12, 39–47.

Brittan, J. N. G. (1980) 'Design for a changing environment', *The Computer Journal*, **23** (1), 13–19.

Budde, R., Kuhlenkamp, K., Mathiassen, L., and Züllighoven, H. (1984) *Approaches to Prototyping*, Springer-Verlag, Berlin.

Cakir, A. (1986) 'Towards an ergonomic design of software', *Behaviour and Information Technology*, **5** (1), 63–70.

Cerveny, R. P. *et al.* (1987) 'Why software prototyping works', *Datamation*, August 15, 97–103.

Giddings, R. V. (1984) 'Accommodating uncertainty in software design', *Communications of the ACM*, **27** (5), May, 428–34.

Gilhooley, I. A. (1984) 'Prototyping', *Systems Development Management*, pp. 1–10, Auerbach Publishers Inc.

Gomaa, H. (1983) 'The impact of rapid prototyping on specifying user requirements', *ACM Software Engineering Notes*, **8** (2), April, 17–28.

Hindle, K. (1984) 'Towards a new development framework', *Data Processing*, **26** (1), January/ February, 6–10.

Janson, M. A. and Douglas Smith, L. D. (1985) 'Prototyping for systems development: a critical appraisal', *MIS Quarterly*, December, 305–16.

Johnson, J. R. (1983) 'A prototypical success story', *Datamation*, Nov., 251–6.

Lantz, K. (1986) 'The prototyping methodology: designing it right the first time', *Computerworld*, April 7, 69–72.

Mason, R. E. A. and Carey, T. T. (1983) 'Prototyping interactive information systems', *Communications of the ACM*, **26** (5), May, 347–54.

McNurlin, B. C. (1981) 'Developing systems by prototyping', *EDP Analyzer*, **19** (9), September, 1–12.

Somogyi, E. K. (1981) 'Prototyping – a method not to be missed', *EDP Analyzer*, October, 13–14.

Swartout, W. and Balzer, R. (1982) 'On the inevitable intertwining of specification and implementation', *Communications of the ACM*, **25** (7), July, 438–40.

Wood-Harper, A. T. and Fitzgerald, G. (1982) 'A taxonomy of current approaches to systems analysis', *The Computer Journal*, **25** (1).

Young, T. R. (1984) 'Superior prototypes, *Datamation*, May 15, 152–8.

CASE

Abbey, S. G. (1984) 'COBOL dumped', *Datamation*, **30** (1), Jan., 108–14.

Canning, R. G. (1981) 'Application system design aids', *EDP Analyzer*, **19** (10), Oct., 1–10.

Case, A. F. (1986) *Information Systems Development: Principles of Computer-Aided Software Engineering*, Prentice Hall, Englewood Cliffs, NJ.

Case, A. F. (1987) 'Evaluating and selecting CASE tools', *CASE Outlook*, **1** (1), July, 6–9.

Connor, A. J. and Case Jr, A. F. (1986) 'Making a case for CASE', *Computerworld*, Special Section: Productivity Software, July 9, 45–6.

Dell, P. W. (1986) 'Early experience with an IPSE', *Software Engineering Journal*, November, 259–64.

Gradwell, D. J. L. (1987) 'Developments in data dictionary standards', *Computer Bulletin*, September, 33–8.

Higgs, M. (1987) 'A clear case', *Computer Weekly*, June 25, 34.

Leavitt, D. (1986) 'Automated development: systems, not just tools', *Software News*, November, 48–58.

Martin, J. and McClure, C. (1985) *Diagramming Techniques for Analysts and Programmers*, Prentice Hall, Englewood Cliffs NJ.

McClure, C. (1987) 'The latest look in programmer productivity tools', *The CASE Report*, October, 1–2.

Merlyn, V. (1987) 'The backlog stops here', *Computerworld*, June 22, 61–4.

Rock-Evans, R. (ed.) (1987) *Analyst Workbenches – State of the Art Report*, Pergamon Infotech, Maidenhead.

Index